HISTORICAL MEMORIAL

OF THE

NEGOTIATION

OF

FRANCE and *ENGLAND*,

From the 26th of MARCH, 1761, to the 20th of SEPTEMBER
of the fame Year,

With the VOUCHERS.

Tranflated from the FRENCH ORIGINAL, publifhed at PARIS by Authority.

LONDON:

Printed for D. WILSON, and T. BECKET and P. A. DEHONDT in the
Strand. M DCC LXI.

First Published 1761
Reprinted 1970

LIBRARY OF CONGRESS CATALOG CARD NUMBER:
73-124790

PRINTED IN THE UNITED STATES OF AMERICA

A N
HISTORICAL MEMORIAL
OF THE
NEGOTIATION
OF
FRANCE and *ENGLAND*.

HIS Majesty thinks it confiftent with his goodnefs and juftice to inform his fubjects of the endeavours he has ufed, and the facrifices he refolved to make, in order to reftore peace to his kingdom.

France, and the whole univerfe, will judge from a plain and faithful detail of the Negotiation, which has been carried on between the Courts of Verfailles and London, which of the two Courts have been averfe to the re-eftablifhment of public tranquillity, and have facrificed the common peace and welfare to their own ambition.

In order to form a clear and juft opinion with regard to the Negotiation which has lately broken off between France and England, it is neceffary to recollect the motives which occafioned the rupture between the two Crowns, and the particular circumftances, which have involved a confiderable part of Europe in a war, which had at firft America only for its object.

The limits of Acadia and Canada, which, by the treaty of Aix-la-Chapelle, were left to the difcuffion of commiffaries to be named by the two Potentates, have ferved England as a pretence for commencing hoftilities, and for taking two French fhips, the *Alcide* and the *Lys*; while, in the midft of peace, and under the fanction of the law of nations, the Duke of Mirepoix, the French Ambaffador, was treating at London in order to prevent a rupture, and to terminate thofe differences, which might have been eafily accommodated at Aix-la-Chapelle, and which, while the peace fubfifted, had met with the moft unreafonable and extravagant oppofition on the part of the Englifh Commiffaries.

The

The unexpected violence offered on the part of the Englifh neceffarily brought on the war : his Majefty found himfelf obliged, though with regret, to repel by force the indignity offered to France, and to prefer the honour of the nation to the tranquillity it enjoyed.

If the court of London had no other defign than to eftablifh the refpective poffeffions of the two Crowns in North America upon a firm footing, fhe would have endeavoured to obviate, as France has done, every incident which might engage the Powers of the Continent of Europe to take part in a war which is abfolutely foreign to them, and which in fact, having no other object but what relates to the limits of Acadia and Canada, could not laft long, and did not require the interpofition of any other Power. But England had more extenfive views : fhe endeavoured to raife a general war againft France, and hoped to renew the famous league which was formed againft Lewis XIV. upon the acceffion of Philip V. to the throne of Spain ; and to perfuade all the Courts of Europe, that they were as much interefted in the limits of Acadia, as in the fucceffion of Charles II.

The conduct of France, in confequence of the firft hoftilities in 1755, was very different from that of England : his Majefty pacified his neighbours, reftrained his Allies, refufed the advantageous profpect of a war, which was propofed to him on the Continent, and gave all the Powers to underftand, that his fole ambition was to reftrain his enemies, the Englifh, within due limits, and to maintain peace and juftice among the Powers, who ought to regard the differences refpecting America with the moft impartial neutrality.

The Court of London, to accomplifh their ends, took advantage of his Majefty's equitable and pacific conduct. She knew that one of the Allies of France might prove a lively obftacle to the eftablifhment of peace and tranquillity, and made no doubt, but, in fecuring that Ally, fhe fhould be able to make that Houfe, which was confidered as the antient rival of France, enter into all her views : but the Emprefs Queen of Hungary and Bohemia, animated by the fame principles of equity of which his Majefty gave fuch laudable proofs, refufed the propofals of England, and rather chofe to run the rifk of an unjuft war, which was the natural and forefeen confequence of the treaty figned at Whitehall between the Kings of England and Pruffia, than to engage in one contrary to the good faith of her Imperial Majefty.

His Majefty and the Emprefs-Queen, previous to the King of Pruffia's invafion of Saxony, entered into an alliance on the 1ft of May 1756, which was purely defenfive. Their Majefties hoped, that their alliance would check the fire which was ready to kindle in Germany, and that it would prevent a war on the Continent of Europe. They were deceived in their expectations : the Court of London had armed the King of Pruffia : nothing could reftrain a Prince whofe paffion for war was unhappily violent : and he began it at the end of the year 1756, by the invafion of Saxony and the attack of Bohemia.

From that time two diftinct wars fubfifted ; one of France with England, and which at the beginning had nothing in common with the war in Germany ; and the other which the King of Pruffia waged againft the Emprefs-Queen, and in which

which the King of Eng'and was interefted as an Ally of the King of Pruffia, and his Majefty, as guarantee of the treaty of Weftphalia, and, after his defenfive treaty of the 1ft of May, as an Ally of the Court of Vienna.

France was cautious, in the engagements fhe was conftrained to make with the Confederate Powers, not to blend the differences which difturbed the peace of America, with thofe which raifed a commotion in Europe. In truth, his Majefty having always made it his principal object to recal each Potentate to terms of reconciliation, and to reftore public tranquillity, he judged it improper to blend interefts of fo diftant and complicated a nature, as thofe of Europe and America would prove, were they to have been jointly treated of in a negotiation for a general and final peace. His Majefty proceeded farther, and with an intent to prevent a direct land war in Europe, he propofed the neutrality of Hanover in the year 1757; the King of England, Elector of Hanover, refufed the propofition, and fent his fon the duke of Cumberland, into his hereditary dominions in Germany, who, at the head of an army entirely compofed of Germans, was ordered to oppofe the march of thofe forces, which his Majefty, in purfuance of his engagements, fent to the affiftance of his Allies who were attacked in their dominions.

The electoral army of Hanover finifhed the campaign of 1757, with the capitulation of *Clofter-Seven.* The Court of London thought proper to break that capitulation, a few months after it had been concluded by the confent of the King of England's fon; the chief pretence alledged was, that the army which had capitulated belonged to the Elector, and that the fame army which, contrary to the right of nations and all military laws, re-entered into action, was from that time to be confidered as a Britifh army. From that moment, (and it is neceffary to attend to this circumftance) the army commanded by Prince Ferdinand of Brunfwick, is become an Englifh army: The Elector of Hanover, the Duke of Brunfwic, the Landgrave of Heffe, their forces and their countries, have been blended together in the caufe of England; fo that the hoftilities in Weftphalia and Lower Saxony have had and ftill have the fame object as the hoftilities in America, Afia and Africa; that is to fay, the difputes fubfifting between the two crowns concerning the limits of Acadia and Canada.

His Majefty confequently from that time being obliged to fupport a war both by fea and land againft England his profeffed enemy, has afforded no farther fuccour of troops to his Allies to enable them to carry on their war in particular, but has only undertaken to preferve the places on the Lower Rhine for the Emprefs Queen, which were acquired by conqueft from the King of Pruffia, in the name of her Imperial Majefty. It would therefore betray ignorance of the moft pofitive facts, to fuppofe that the war which is actually carried on in Weftphalia, is for the intereft of his Majefty's Allies; that war is purely Englifh, which is carried on only becaufe the army of England, in that part, defends the poffeffions of the King of Great Britain and his Allies.

We muft conclude from what has been faid with regard to the ftate of the two Belligerant Crowns, that the war of France with England is in fact, and in its origin, very diftinct from that of the Emprefs againft the King of Pruffia: neverthevertheleſs there is a connection between the two wars, which conſiſts in the common engagement between the King and the Empreſs Queen, not to make a ſeparate peace with the common enemy but by mutual conſent. This engagement, which is ſo conformable to the ſentiments of friendſhip and confidence by which their Majeſties are united, was neceſſary for their reciprocal ſecurity. As it would be dangerous for the forces of the King of Pruſſia to join againſt France, with thoſe of England, commanded by Prince Ferdinand, it would be equally prejudicial and contrary to the faith of his Majeſty's engagements with the Court of Vienna, that the Britiſh army ſhould join the King of Pruſſia againſt the Empreſs Queen, and againſt the Princes of the Empire who are in alliance with France.

Although the year 1758, produced no political event, which might give room to a negotiation for the re-eſtabliſhment of peace, yet France, ever zealous to promote it with the ſame ſincerity, made uſe of the mediation of Denmark to inform England of her perſeverance in the ſame pacific diſpoſitions; the anſwer from the Court of London was as haughty as it was negative, and deſtroyed all hopes of a negotiation.

In 1759, the Courts of London and Berlin tranſmitted the following declaration from the Hague, to the Miniſters of France, Vienna and Ruſſia.

No. I.

Declaration of their Pruſſian and Britannic Majeſties.

' THEIR Britannic and Pruſſian Majeſties, touched with compaſſion, when
' they reflect on the evils which have been occaſioned, and muſt ſtill neceſ-
' ſarily reſult from the war which has been kindled for ſome years paſt, would
' think themſelves wanting to the duties of humanity, and particularly regard-
' leſs of the intereſt they take in the preſervation and welfare of their reſpective
' kingdoms and ſubjects, if they neglected to uſe proper meaſures towards check-
' ing the progreſs of this cruel peſtilence, and to contribute towards the re-eſtab-
' liſhment of public tranquillity. It is with this view, and in order to aſcertain
' the ſincerity of their intentions in this reſpect, that their aforeſaid Majeſties have
' reſolved to make the following declaration :

' That they are ready to ſend Plenipotentiaries to any place which ſhall be
' judged moſt convenient, in order to treat, in conjunction, concerning a general
' and firm peace, with thoſe whom the Belligerant Powers ſhall think proper to
' authorize on their ſide, towards the accompliſhment of ſo ſalutary an end.

' I certify, that the above Declaration is the ſame which was diſpatched to
' me by the Earl of Holderneſſe and the Baron Kniphauzen, in the name, and
' on the part of their Britannic and Pruſſian Majeſties.'

Given at the Caſtle of Ryſwick, this 25th November 1759.

Signed L. D. de Brunſwick.

This declaration made no mention either of Sweden, or of the King of Poland, Elector of Saxony, two Powers who were principally intereſted in the war.

France

France and her Allies were not aware of this proceeding of the courts of London and Berlin. They were obliged to wait for an anſwer from Peterſbourg, in order to tranſmit in common a counter declaration, which the great diſtance between the countries obliged them to defer longer than France could have wiſhed. At length it was tranſmitted in the following terms, and the Courts of London and Berlin never made any reply to it.

No. II.

Counter Declaration of His Moſt Chriſtian Majeſty.

'THEIR Britannic and Pruſſian Majeſties having thought proper to teſtify,
' by a Declaration which was delivered on their parts at the Hague, the
' 25th of November laſt, to the Ambaſſadors and Miniſters of the Courts of
' Verſailles, Vienna, and Peterſbourg, reſident with their High Mightineſſes the
' States General of the United Provinces, that, from a ſincere deſire of contri-
' buting to the re-eſtabliſhment of public tranquillity, they were ready to ſend
' Plenipotentiaries to any place which ſhould be judged moſt convenient, in or-
' der to treat concerning that important objeʼct with thoſe whom the Belligerent
' Powers ſhould think proper to authorize on their parts, for the accompliſh-
' ment of ſo ſalutary an end.

' His Majeſty the Moſt Chriſtian King, her Majeſty the Empreſs Queen of
' Hungary and Bohemia, and her Majeſty the Empreſs of all the Ruſſias, be-
' ing equally animated with a deſire of contributing to the re-eſtabliſhment of
' public tranquillity, on a juſt and ſolid footing, do declare in return,

' That his Majeſty the Catholic King having been pleaſed to offer his media-
' tion with reſpect to the war, which has ſubſiſted ſome years between France
' and England ; and this war having no objeʼct in common with that which has
' likewiſe for ſome years been carried on by the two Empreſſes with their Allies,
' againſt the King of Pruſſia ;

' His Moſt Chriſtian Majeſty is ready to enter into a treaty of peace with
' England, ſo far as it regards himſelf, through the good offices of his Catholic
' Majeſty, whoſe mediation he accepts with pleaſure.

' With reſpect to the war which directly concerns his Pruſſian Majeſty, their
' Majeſties the Moſt Chriſtian King, the Empreſs Queen of Hungary and Bo-
' hemia, and the Empreſs of all the Ruſſias, are diſpoſed to co operate towards
' the appointment of the propoſed congreſs ; but as, by virtue of their treaties,
' they cannot enter into any engagements relative to peace, but in conjunction
' with their Allies, it will be neceſſary, in order that they may explain them-
' ſelves preciſely on this ſubject, that their Britannic and Pruſſian Majeſties.
' would firſt be pleaſed to ſend their invitation to the Congreſs, to all the Pow-
' ers who are directly at war with the King of Pruſſia, particularly his Majeſty
' of Sweden, as well as his Poliſh Majeſty Elector of Saxony, who ought to be
' expreſly invited to the future Congreſs.'

8

In

In this Counter Declaration, France expresly separated her particular war with England, whether in Africa, Asia, America, or in Westphalia, from the war which was carried on in Saxony and Silesia. The King of Spain had then offered his good offices to bring about a reconciliation between France and England. The separation of the two wars, and the tender which his Catholic Majesty made of his good offices, induced the King to hope that the separate peace of France might be successfully negociated at the Court of London. In consequence of this expectation, he ordered the Count D'Affry, his Majesty's Ambassador at the Hague, to enter into a conference with General Yorke, the Envoy Extraordinary from the King of Great Britain. Those two Ministers had several conferences, which evidently proved that the Court of London was extremely averse to an accommodation, and that the Declaration, which she caused to be transmitted by Prince Lewis of Brunswick (to put the most favourable construction on it) was no more than an external act of complaisance for her Allies, and that she absolutely never intended it should take effect.

His Majesty was not discouraged by the inflexibility he still experienced on the part of his enemies, from endeavouring to bring about a just accommodation. His Majesty, in 1761, thought proper to declare his sentiments, and pacific inclinations to his allies. He found them inclined to concur in any measures which might facilitate and accelerate the re-establishment of public peace, and in consequence of these salutary dispositions, all the Confederate Powers agreed to tranimit the following declaration to London.

No. III.

The Declaration of his Most Christian Majesty.

' THE pacific dispositions which the Kings of England and Prussia ex-
' pressed the last year, and which are conformable to the sentiments of
' all the Belligerant Powers, having met with some difficulties which have
' proved obstacles to their success, the Courts of France, Vienna, Petersburg,
' Stockholm and Warsaw, have unanimously agreed to invite those of London
' and Berlin, to the renewal of a Negotiation so expedient for the welfare of
' mankind, and which ought to interest all the powers at war in the cause of
' humanity.

' With this view, and in order to proceed towards the re-establishment of
' peace, they propose the meeting of a Congress, at which they think it will be
' convenient to admit, with the Plenipotentiaries of the principal Belligerant
' Powers, no other than those of their Allies. If the Kings of England and
' Prussia adopt this measure, his Most Christian Majesty, the Empress Queen,
' the Empress of Russia, the King of Sweden, and the King of Poland Elector
' of Saxony, propose the town of Augsburg, as the place of Congress, which
' they only point out as a town within the reach of all the parties interested,
' which by its situation seems to suit the convenience of all the States, and
' they will not oppose the choice of any other town in Germany, which their
' Britannic and Prussian Majesties may deem more convenient.

' His

' His Most Christian Majesty, the Empress Queen, the Empress of Russia,
' and the Kings of Sweden and Poland, declare farther, that they have made
' choice of Plenipotentiaries, to whom they will commit their interests at the
' Congress, in expectation that the King of England, the King of Prussia,
' and their Allies, will speedily make choice of their respective Ministers, that
' the Negotiation may not be retarded.

' The sincerity of this declaration, which the Courts of France, Vienna, Pe-
' tersburg, Stockholm, and Warsaw have, out of regard to the general good,
' determined to make to the Courts of London and Berlin, gives them to hope
' that their Britannic and Prussian Majesties, will signify, by a speedy answer,
' their sentiments on a subject, so essential to the peace and welfare of Europe.

' By order, and in the name of his Most Christian Majesty,

' Signed, the Duke de Choiseul."

This declaration, which concerned all the Allies in general, was not sufficient to put a stop to the miseries of war, so speedily as France could have wished.

In fact, what delays and perplexing incidents were not to be expected from a Congress at which the interests of America were to be treated of at the same time with those of the two Empresses, Sweden, Saxony, and the King of Prussia!

To remove these obstacles, the King, with the consent of his Allies, thought proper to press for a separation of the two wars, which had been agreed upon since the year 1759. In consequence of this intention, his Majesty caused a separate Memorial to be addressed to the Court of London, which was accompanied by a letter from the Duke de Choiseul, his Minister and Secretary of State for foreign affairs, to Mr. Pitt, Minister and Secretary of State to his Britannic Majesty.

No. IV.

Letter from the Duke de Choiseul to Mr. Pitt.

SIR,

' THE King my Master, acting in conformity with the sentiments of his Al-
' lies, in order, if possible, to procure the re-establishment of a general
' peace, has authorized me to transmit to your Excellency the Memorial here-
' to annexed, which solely concerns the interests of France and England, with
' respect to the particular war between the two Crowns. The King has reason
' to hope, that the sincere manner in which he proposes to treat with his
' Britannic Majesty, will banish all mistrust in the course of the Negotiation,
' if it takes place, and will induce his Britannic Majesty to make the King ac-
' quainted with his real sentiments, whether with regard to the continuance of
' war, or with respect to the conclusion of peace, as well as in relation to the
' principles on which they ought to proceed, in order to procure this blessing to
' the two nations.

B

' I will

' I will add, that I am likewife authorized to affure your Excellency, that
' in relation to the war in which the King of Pruffia is concerned, the Allies of
' the King my Mafter are determined to treat of their interefts in the future
' Congrefs, with the fame franknefs and fincerity, of which I can give your Ex-
' cellency affurance on the part of France ; and that, fo as not to depart from
' what is due to their dignity, their fituation, and to the demands of juftice,
' they will bring with them to the Negotiation all the acquiefcence, which
' their humanity dictates for the general good of Europe.

' The King my Mafter, and his Allies, do not doubt but that they fhall
' find the heart of his Britannic Majefty and his Allies, impreffed with the
' fame fentiments. I efteem it a happinefs that my office makes me the inftru-
' ment of conveying fuch favourable fentiments, which give me an opportuni-
' ty of affuring your Excellence, with what diftinguifhed confideration I have
' the honour to be, &c.

No. V.

Memorial of the Chriftian King.

' THE Moft Chriftian King wifhes that the feparate peace of France with
' England could be united with the general peace of Europe, which his
' Majefty moft fincerely defires to eftablifh ; but as the nature of the objects
' which have occafioned the war between France and England, is totally fo-
' reign from the difputes in Germany, his Moft Chriftian Majefty has thought
' it neceffary to agree with his Britannic Majefty on the principal articles which
' may form the bafis of their feparate Negotiations, in order to accelerate, as
' much as poffible, the general conclufion of the peace.

' The beft method to accomplifh the end propofed, is to remove thofe in-
' tricacies which might prove obftacles to its fuccefs. In the bufinefs of peace,
' the difputes of nations concerning their reciprocal conquefts, the different opi-
' nions with refpect to the utility of particular conquefts, and the compenfations for
' reftitutions, generally form matter of embarraffment at a Negotiation of peace. As
' it is natural for each nation, with regard to thefe different points, to endeavour
' the acquifition of all poffible advantages, intereft and diftruft occafion oppofitions
' and produce delays. To obviate thefe inconveniencies, and to teftify the fin-
' cerity of his proceedings in the courfe of the Negotiation of peace with Eng-
' land, the Moft Chriftian King propofes to agree with his Britannic Majefty,
' that, with refpect to the particular war of France and England, the two Crowns
' fhall remain in poffeffion of what they have conquered from each other, and
' that the fituation in which they fhall ftand on the 1ft of September, in the
' year 1761, in the Eaft Indies, on the 1ft of July in the fame year, in the
' Weft Indies and in Africa, and on the 1ft of May following in Europe, fhall
' be the pofition which fhall ferve as a bafis to the treaty which may be nego-
' tiated between the two powers. Which fhews that the Moft Chriftian King, in
' in order to fet an example of humanity, and to contribute to the re-eftablifh-
' ment of the general tranquillity, will make a facrifice of thofe reftitutions
' which

‘ which he has a right to claim, at the same time that he will maintain those
‘ acquisitions which he has gained from England during the course of the
‘ war.

‘ Nevertheless as his Britannic Majesty may think that the periods proposed of
‘ the 1st of September, July, and May, are either too near or too distant for
‘ the interests of the British Crown, or that his Britannic Majesty may judge
‘ it proper to make compensation for the whole, or for part of the reciprocal con-
‘ quests of the two Crowns, the Most Christian King will readily enter into Ne-
‘ gotiation with his Britannic Majesty in relation to these two objects, when he
‘ shall know his sentiments concerning them, the principal view of his Most
‘ Christian Majesty, being to testify not only to England, but to the whole
‘ world, his sincere disposition to remove all impediments which might defer the
‘ salutary object of peace.

‘ The Most Christian King expects, that the disposition of his Britannic Ma-
‘ jesty will be correspondent, and that he will, with equal sincerity, answer all
‘ the articles contained in this Memorial, in which the two Powers are so essen-
‘ tially interested.”

These pieces were dated the 26th of March. England had then conquered
from France Isle Royal or Cape Breton, all Canada, the Isles of Guadaloupe and
Marigalant, and that of Goree in Africa, with Senegal; Europe at that time
was ignorant of the precise situation of affairs between the two Crowns in Asia,
and the expedition against Belle-Isle had not then taken place.

France, on the other hand, had conquered the Island of Minorca, had repaired
some parts of the port of Dunkirk, and in Germany were in possession of Hanau,
the Langraviate of Hesse, and the town of Gottingen in the Electorate of Hanover. It is necessary to observe, that Cassel was besieged on the 26th of March,
and that it was to be feared that on the 1st of May the King’s forces would no
longer be in possession of Hesse, and of the town of Gottingen.

Wesel and Gueldres could not be comprised in the offer of *Uti possidetis* which
France proposed, because those two towns, and the countries dependant on
them, appertain to the Empress-Queen: that the King has only the custody of
them, and that justice is administred there in the name of her Imperial Majesty.

All Europe was astonished at the sacrifices which the King was disposed to
make to England: his Majesty’s Ministry were reproached on the part of those
Courts who were most affectionate to France, and no one doubted but that England would prefer the quiet possession of her conquests, and the repose of her
Allies in Germany, to the continuation of the war. The memorial of France,
by establishing a fixed basis for the Negociation, proposed to make necessary compensations for the advantage of the two crowns, and opened a way for the evacuation of Germany on the part of the French troops, in compensation of the
conquests of England in America.

The full extent of the proposition contained in the Memorial of the 26th of
March, addressed to Mr. Pitt, was known in France; but the King, like a true
Father of his people, thought of nothing but their relief; and in consequence of
this

this sentiment, determined to adhere to the offers which seemed to him the most sure and ready expedients for inspiring his enemies with that spirit of reconciliation, which directed all his Majesty's wishes and measures.

Mr. Pitt answered the Duke of Choiseul's Letter, and at the same time sent him a Memorial, in answer to that of France of the 26th of March.

No. VI.

Mr. Pitt's Letter to the Duke of Choiseul.

S I R,   *London,* 8th *April,* 1761.

' THE King my Master has authorized me to transmit to your Excellency, with all the dispatch which was found possible, the Memorial hereto annexed, in answer to that of the 26th of the last month, made by the order and in the name of his Most Christian Majesty, solely concerning the interests of England and France, relative to the particular war between the two Crowns, which was accompanied by a letter from your Excellency of the same date, transmitted to me by M. the Prince Galitzin.

' His Majesty has published his real sentiments, with regard to the salutary business of Peace, with the sincerity which his Christian Majesty desires, and of which he himself set the example; the king my Master, on his part, desires nothing more than, by the sincerity of his conduct, to remove all distrust in course of the Negociation.

' I will likewise acquaint your Excellency, that the King learnt with great satisfaction, that your Excellency was authorized to give assurance that, in relation to the war which concerns the King of Prussia, the Allies of his Most Christian Majesty are determined to treat with the same openness and sincerity as the Court of France, and that they will bring with them, to the Negociation at the future Congress, all the acquiescence which their unanimity dictates for the general good of Europe.

' I must add that, with regard to the war which concerns the King of Prussia, as well as with respect to the other Allies of the King my Master, his Majesty, always constant in fulfilling the engagements of his crown with the most scrupulous exactness, can never fail to support their respective interests, whether in the course of the Negociation, (which may God prosper) or in the continuance of the war, (if contrary to all expectation this misfortune should be unavoidable) with the cordiality and efficacy of a sincere and faithful Ally.

' As to what remains, it is superfluous to mention to what degree his Majesty wishes for this speedy establishment of the general peace in Germany, after the distinguished proof his Majesty has given, in so readily consenting to the proposition of so distant a place as the town of Augsbourg for the meeting of the Congress.

Such

' Such are the fincere and upright intentions of the King my Mafter for the re-
' eftablifhment of the public tranquility. I think myfelf happy in having the
' charge of conveying fuch fentiments, and of having an opportunity of affuring
' your Excellency of the diftinguifhed regard with which I have the honour to
' be, &c.

Signed W. Pitt.

No. VII.

The Memorial of his Britannic Majefty, of the 8th of April 1761.

' HIS Britannic Majefty, equally defirous with the Moft Chriftian King, that
' the feparate Peace of England and France could be united with the gene-
' ral peace, for which the King of Great Britain is fo fincerely interefted, that,
' in regard to this point, he even means that the contefts which might arife be-
' tween the two Crowns concerning their particular differences, fhould not occa-
' fion the leaft delay to the fpeedy conclufion of fo falutary a work as the general
' peace of Germany ; and his Britannic Majefty is the more confirmed in this
' fentiment, dictated by humanity towards fo many nations, that he feels in all
' its extent the propofition which the Moft Chriftian King eftablifhes as a funda-
' mental principle ; that the nature of the objects which have occafioned the war
' between England and France, is totally foreign from the difputes in Ger-
' many.

' In confequence of this inconteftible principle, the King of Great Britain en-
' tirely adopts the fentiment of his Moft Chriftian Majefty, that it is neceffary to
' agree between the two Crowns on fome principal articles, which may form the
' bafis of their particular negociations, in order the more to accelerate the con-
' clufion of a general peace.'

' The King of Great Britain equally agrees in general to the propofition which
' the Moft Chriftian King has made with an opennefs, in which his Britannic
' Majefty will concur throughout the courfe of the negotiation ; that is to fay,
' that, in relation to the particular war between England and France, 1. The
' two Crowns fhall remain in poffeffion of what they have conquered, one from
' the other. 2. That the fituation in which they fhall ftand at certain periods,
' fhall be the pofition to ferve as a bafis for the Treaty which may be negociated
' between the two Powers.

' With regard to the firft branch of the aforefaid propofition, his Britannic Ma-
' jefty takes pleafure in doing juftice to the magnanimity of His Moft Chriftian
' Majefty, who, from motives of humanity, determines to facrifice to the love
' of peace, the reftitution which he thinks he has a right to claim, maintaining
' at the fame time what he has conquered from England during the courfe of
' the war.

' With refpect to the fecond head of the aforefaid propofition, concerning
' the reciprocal Conquefts made by the two Crowns one upon another ; that is to
' fay, That the fituation in which they fhall ftand at the refpective periods af-
' figned

7

'signed for the different quarters of the globe, shall serve as a basis for the said
'Treaty, the King of Great Britain again acknowledges with satisfaction the
'candour which is manifested on the part of his Most Christian Majesty in this
'article, by obviating, as he has done, the extreme difficulties, and by antici-
'pating the indispensable objections, which could not but arise on such a sub-
'ject; it being in fact self-evident, that expeditions at sea requiring preparati-
'ons of long standing, and depending on navigations which are uncertain, as
'well as on the concurrence of seasons, in places which are often too distant for
'orders relative to their execution to be adapted to the common vicissitudes of
'negociations, which for the most part are subject to disappointments and de-
'lays, and are always fluctuating and precarious : from whence it necessarily re-
'sults, that the nature of such operations is by no means susceptible, without pre-
'judice to the party who employs them, of any other epochas, than those which
'have reference to the day of signing the treaty of peace.

'Nevertheless as this consideration, as well as that which respects the Com-
'pensations (if such shall be found proper to be made between the two Crowns)
'on account of their reciprocal Conquests, comprehend the most interesting and
'capital articles of the Treaty, and as it is upon these two decisive objects, that
'the Most Christian King voluntarily offers to enter into a Negociation ; the King
'of Great Britain, desiring to concur effectually with the favourable dispositions
'of the Most Christian King, in order to remove all impediments, which might
'defer the salutary object of peace, his Brittannic Majesty declares that he is
'ready on his part to enter upon the proposed Negotiation with speed and sincerity.
'And more authentically to demonstrate to what extent the sincerity of his con-
'duct proceeds, his Britannic Majesty declares farther, that he should be glad
'to see some person at London sufficiently authorized, by a power from the Most
'Christian King, to enter upon this subject with the British Ministers, in re-
'gard to the several articles contained in the Letter of the D. de Choiseul of
'the 26th of March 1761, to the Secretary of State of his Britannic Majesty,
'which points are so essentially interesting to the two Powers.

'By the order, and in the name of the King of Great Britain my Master,

Signed W. Pitt.

The Letter of the English Minister shews, in appearance, an equal zeal with
that of France, for the re-establishment of the Union between the two Crowns :
it contains, moreover, a declaration in favour of the King of Prussia, which
seems foreign to the purpose, and appears the more affected, as the King never
testified the least desire to separate the alliance which united England to his Prussian Majesty.

The British Memorial, annexed to the letter of the English Minister, accepts
the *Statu Quo*, but says nothing with regard to the epochas. In fact, it is concluding nothing with regard to that interesting and necessary object attached to
the proposition of *Uti Possidetis*, to say that the peace shall be the epoch to fix
the possessions of the two powers.

In

In the conclusion, England proposed the sending of a French Minister to London. This proposition gave a favourable omen of the dispositions of the British Court towards peace. The King ordered the D. de Choiseul to return an answer to Mr. Pitt, and to accompany it with a Memorial which, at the same time that it clearly expressed his Majesty's real sentiments, contained an acceptance of the proposal for sending a Minister to London, which required the reciprocality of dispatching an English Minister to France.

No. VIII.

Letter from the D. de Choiseul to Mr. Pitt.

S I R, Versailles, 19th April, 1761.

' I Made the King my master acquainted with the letter which your Excellency
' did me the honour to write to me on the 8th instant, as well as with the
' Memorial thereto annexed.

' His Majesty has remarked with real pleasure, the conformity of his Britan-
' nic Majesty's sentiments with his own, in regard to the sincere and open con-
' duct which it becomes two such great Powers to observe in the Negotiation of
' a Peace.

' The King has not delayed, Sir, the nomination of an Ambassador to re-
' present him at the Congress at Augsburg. His Majesty has made choice of
' the Count de Choiseul, at present his Ambassador at Vienna, and he will re-
' pair to the town appointed, at the beginning of July, in the expectation which
' we entertain here, that his Britannic Majesty will send his Ambassador thither
' at the same time.

' The King has commanded me, Sir, to observe on this occasion to your
' Excellency, in answer to the declaration contained in your letter, that his Ma-
' jesty, as constant as any other Power, in fulfilling the engagements he, has
' made with the Allies with the most scrupulous punctuality, will continue, with
' that fidelity which is consistent with the integrity and dignity of his character, to
' make his cause common with theirs, whether in the negotiation for the peace
' of Germany, or in the continuance of the war, if, to the misfortune of man-
' kind, the favourable dispositions in which the Belligerent Powers are at present
' should not be attended with the success which is so earnestly desired.

' I ought not, on this occasion, to omit informing your Excellency with what
' concern the King would see himself obliged to continue such a destructive war,
' after having entertained a confidence that all the parties were interested in put-
' ting a stop to the calamities it occasions.

' As to what relates to the war in particular between France and England, I
' have annexed to this letter a Memorial in reply to that of your Excellency.
' We cannot be too zealous in explaining the upright intentions of our Masters, in
' order to remove, at the beginning of this interesting negotiation, those misun-
' derstandings, which often augment, instead of lessening the delay.

' You are a Minister, Sir, too enlightened, not to approve of this principle.

' I have the honour to be, with most distinguished regard, &c.

' Signed Le Duc de Choiseul.'

No. IX.

No. IX.

The Memorial of his Most Christian Majesty of the 19th April, 1761.

‘ THE Most Christian King perceives with satisfaction, that his Britannic
‘ Majesty agrees that the nature of the objects which have occasioned the
‘ war between France and England is totally foreign from the disputes which
‘ have given rise to the war in Germany; it is in consequence of this principle
‘ that his Most Christian Majesty offered the King of England to treat concern-
‘ ing the preliminaries relative to the particular interests of the two Crowns;
‘ but in making that proposition, the King of France, did not understand, as
‘ the beginning of the Memorial of London of the 8th of April seems to inti-
‘ mate, that the peace of Germany could take place, without the differences
‘ between France and England being adjusted. His Most Christian Majesty has
‘ sufficient confidence in his Allies to be certain that they will neither conclude
‘ a peace nor a treaty, without his consent. He did not understand therefore,
‘ that the peace of Germany could be concluded distinctly from that of France
‘ and England, and he only proposed to the King of England, to separate the
‘ discussion of the two wars, in order to bring about a general peace for all
‘ parties.
‘ His Most Christian Majesty renews the proposition which he caused to be
‘ made in the first Memorial, that the two Powers should remain in *Statu Quo*
‘ with regard to their possessions and conquests, according to the periods stated
‘ in the said Memorial, but his Majesty observes, that the basis of the propo-
‘ sition is necessarily connected with the epochas proposed; for it is easy to con-
‘ ceive that such events may happen on either side, as may absolutely prevent an
‘ acquiescence to the *Uti Possidetis*, if the epochas are distant; and his Most Christian
‘ Majesty has the more reason to recal the whole proposition, if the King of En-
‘ gland does not acquiesce to the epochas annexed to it, since no one can doubt
‘ but that those periods were proposed at a time when they were not advantage-
‘ ous to France.
‘ It is certain that the reciprocal conquests cannot be ascertained but on the
‘ day of signing the peace; but it is no less certain, that it is impossible to fix
‘ the basis of a negotiation for peace, otherwise than according to the situation
‘ in which the Belligerant Parties stood at such or such a period of the war.
‘ This is the light in which the King of France understood the proposition which
‘ he made to the King of England; and it is upon this principle, if his Britannic
‘ Majesty adopts it, that his Most Christian Majesty will send a Minister to Lon-
‘ don with credentials, and charged with full power sufficient to treat with the
‘ Ministers of the King of Great Britain, either with respect to the ground of the
‘ dispute, or in regard to the compensations proper to be made to the two Crowns,
‘ as well as concerning the interests of their colonies and their commerce.
‘ The disposition of his Most Christian Majesty, to put an end to the mise-
‘ ries of war, which divides the two nations under their government, is equal to
‘ that of his Britannic Majesty; but as the zeal on both sides should be alike,
‘ at the same time that the Most Christian King shall send M. Bussy to London,

‘ he

' he hopes that the King of Great Britain will fend an Englifh Minifter to France,
' to treat concerning the fame objects with his Miniftry. His Moft Chriftian
' Majefty expects the anfwer of his Britannic Majefty on the contents of this Me-
' morial, in order to expedite and receive the reciprocal and neceffary paffports.
         ' By the order and in the name of the King my Mafter,
                        ' Signed Le Duc de Choifeul.'

Mr. Pitt's anfwer contained a new Memorial on the part of England, in which
their arguments with refpect to the epochs were far from being juft : for, altho'
France propofed, by the Memorial of the 26th of March, to negotiate with refpect to the epochs, it was not the lefs certain, that the propofition of *Uti poffide-*
dis was connected with thofe epochs, whether the Courts agreed that they fhould
be diftant or near. In fact, if it fhould happen that they could not agree in that
particular, it was evident that the propofition of *Uti poffidetis* dropped with the
Negotiation.

No. X.

Mr. Pitt's letter to the Duke de Choifeul.

MONSIEUR,   *Whiteball,* 28th *April,* 1761.
' I Have laid before the King my mafter the letter which your Excellency did
'   me the honour to write to me the 19th of this month, as alfo the Memo-
' rial which was annexed to it.
  ' His Majefty fincerely wifhes to maintain an entire conformity of fentiments
' with his Moft Chriftian Majefty, in relation to the uniform and direct method
' which it is proper to purfue in a Negotiation equally delicate and important.
  ' The King underftands, Sir, with pleafure, that his Moft Chriftian Majefty
' has made choice of the Count de Choifeul to reprefent him at the Congrefs at
' Augfburg, and that that Ambaffador will repair to the deftined town at the be-
' ginning of July ; and the King has charged me to inform your Excellency, that
' he has nominated the Earl of Egremont, Lord Vifcount Stormont, and Sir
' Jofeph York, to reprefent him at the faid Congrefs, and that his Ambaffadors
' will likewife repair to Augfburg at the beginning of July.
  ' It becomes me, on this fubject, to acquaint your Excellency, that the re-
' gret of the King my mafter would not be lefs than that of the Moft Chriftian
' King, to fee the war continued in Germany, which is deftructive to fo many
' nations.
  ' I annex to this letter a Memorial, in anfwer to that of your Excellency of
' the 19th inftant, in relation to the war in particular between Great Britain and
' France. It is true, Sir, the principle of removing mifunderftandings in bufi-
' nefs, upon all occafions, cannot be too highly approved ; therefore it cannot
' efcape the obfervation of your Excellency, that at the beginning of an accom-
' modation, unexpected alterations naturally have the effect of involving the over-
' tures in obfcurity and uncertainty, rather than of introducing that perfpicuity
' and confidence, fo indifpenfable in a Negotiation between two fuch great
                    C   ' Powers.

'Powers. As the natural remedy againſt inconveniences of this nature ſeems to
' be the preſence of reciprocal Miniſters, who, treating by word of mouth, may
' give an explanation immediately on ſtarting of a doubt, your Excellency will
' ſee by the Memorial hereto annexed, the diſpoſition of his Majeſty in this
' reſpect.

 ' I have the honour to be, with the moſt diſtinguiſhed regard, &c.

' Signed W. Pitt.'

No. XI.

The Memorial of his Britannic Majeſty of the 28th of April, 1761.

'THE King of Great Britain, always influenced by the ſame deſire of putting
' an end to the miſeries of the war, which is unhappily kindled between
' Great Britain and France, has with pleaſure concurred in every meaſure which
' tends to remove the obſtacles which impede ſo ſalutary a work. It is with this
' view, that his Britannic Majeſty will readily ſend Mr. Stanley to France, in
' the quality of his Miniſter, at the ſame time that the Moſt Chriſtian King ſhall
' ſend Mr. Buſſy to London.

' As to what remains, his Majeſty does not find by the Memorial of the 26th
' of laſt month, made in the name of his Moſt Chriſtian Majeſty, that the ground
' of the propoſition therein contained, concerning the reciprocal conqueſts, is ne-
' ceſſarily connected with the periods propoſed ; quite on the contrary ; it is
' expreſsly about thoſe very periods that the Moſt Chriſtian King offers to enter
' into a Negotiation. Theſe are the expreſs words : *Neverthelefs, as his Majeſty*
' *may think that the propoſed periods of September, July, and May, may be either*
' *too near or too diſtant for the intereſts of the Britiſh Crown, or that his Britannic*
' *Majeſty ſhould think proper that compenſation ſhould be made for the whole or part*
' *of the reciprocal conqueſts of the two Crowns ; upon theſe two points, the Moſt*
' *Chriſtian King will readily enter into a Negotiation with his Britannic Majeſty,*
' *when he ſhall be acquainted with his intentions.*

' It was in conſequence of an offer ſo clearly expreſſed, and not capable of miſ-
' conſtruction, that his Britannic Majeſty reſolved to declare, that he was ready
' on his part to enter, with ſpeed and ſincerity, upon the propoſed Negotiation.
' The King of Great Britain, perſevering in his intentions, renews his former
' declaration ; and his Britannic Majeſty, to leave no doubt with regard to his
' inclinations, has forwarded the paſſport hereto annexed, and will be glad to
' receive one immediately in return from the Court of France, that, by means of
' a treaty by word of mouth, as well with reſpect to the grounds of the diſpute,
' as in relation to the epochs, as alſo in regard to the compenſation which may
' be agreed on between the two Crowns, they may be better able on both ſides
' to clear up doubts, and remove all ambiguities from the Negotiation, which,
' in order to be effectual, ſhould be conducted on both ſides with ſincerity, pre-
' ciſion and expedition.

 ' By the order, and in the name of the King, my Maſter,

' Signed W. Pitt.'

I.

The

The paſſports for Mr. Buſſy being arrived, the King ordered thoſe neceſſary for Mr. Stanley to be expedited, and the diſpatch of the reſpective Miniſters for the important Negotiation on foot, was ſettled by the Letters here annexed.

No. XII.

Letter from the D. de Choiſeul to Mr. Pitt.

S I R,

' THE King, my Maſter, entirely adopts the principle advanced in the letter
' with which your Excellency honoured me on the 28th of laſt Month, as
' likewiſe in the Memorial thereto annexed, with reſpect to the neceſſity of diſ-
' patching reſpective Miniſters, in order to elucidate a number of difficulties,
' which it is impoſſible to obviate by letters and memorials. I ſhould never-
' theleſs have been proud of the honour of negotiating ſo important an affair
' perſonally with your Excellency. No one has a higher confidence than myſelf
' in the integrity and the uncommon talents which your Excellency poſſeſſes, and
' I do preſume, that the intentions of the Kings, our Maſters, being at once de-
' termined on peace, the ſagacity of your Excellency, joined to my zeal for ſo
' precious a bleſſing, would have ſmoothed all difficulties; but as our employs
' neceſſarily keep us at a diſtance from a perſonal Negotiation, M. de Buſſy,
' who is uſed to tranſact buſineſs with me, will ſupply, near your Excellency,
' the deſire I have of concurring in the ſalutary views of peace, which ſeem to
' animate all the belligerent Powers. I entreat your Excellency to grant him
' your favour, and I am certain that he will uſe his utmoſt endeavours to de-
' ſerve it.

' Your Excellency will ſee by my private letter, to which his Majeſty's paſſ-
' ports for Mr. Stanley are annexed, ſome precautionary arrangements, which I
' propoſe to be ſettled, in order to prevent the inconveniences which might ariſe
' on the firſt diſpatch of the reſpective Miniſters.

' I have the honour to be, &c.

' Signed Le Duc de Choiſeul.'

No. XIII.

Another Letter from the D. de Choiſeul to Mr. Pitt, of the 4th May, 1761.

' I Have received the paſſport of the King of Great Britain, which your Excel-
' lency did me the honour to ſend for M. Buſſy, in the quality of Miniſter
' of the King, my Maſter; and I ſend you in return his Majeſty's paſſport for
' Mr. Stanley, whom his Britannic Majeſty has been pleaſed to appoint in order
' to come to this Court in the ſame capacity. I think it my duty, on this occa-
' ſion, Sir, to make ſome obſervations, which ſeem to me neceſſary to warrant
' the execution of the commiſſions of thoſe two Miniſters.

1. ' The King thinks, that his Britannic Majeſty will judge it convenient that
' the two Miniſters ſhould be charged with full power from the reſpective Courts
' to uſe upon occaſion.

C 2   2. ' That

2. ' That the two Ministers should each of them have Letters of Credence
' from the Kings, their Masters, which they shall deliver to the respective Se-
' cretaries of State only ; that is to say, in France, to the Minister and Secretary
' of State for the department of Foreign Affairs; and in England, to the Mini-
' ster and Secretary of State for the Southern Department.

3. ' As his Majesty's intention is, that the English Minister shall enjoy the
' same privilege in France, as if the two Courts were in the midst of peace, as
' well with regard to the common intercourse of life, as in maintaining a corre-
' spondence with the Court of England and the other Courts of Europe, and
' lastly, for the dispatch of his couriers, and with respect to all the prerogatives
' and franchises in general incident to his character ; his Majesty relies, that
' M. Bussy will absolutely enjoy the same rights, prerogatives, franchises and
' liberties, at London ; it being understood nevertheless, that when one or the
' other are about to dispatch their couriers to their own or any other Court, they
' shall be obliged to require a passport from the Secretary of State in the depart-
' ment, which shall not be refused to them, any more than the necessary vessel
' to transport their couriers from France to England, and from England to
' France.

4. ' We desire to know when Mr. Stanley will be ready to leave London
' in order to repair to Calais, in order to direct M. Bussy's journey, so that he
' may repair to Calais at the same time, to be transported to England in the same
' vessel which brings Mr. Stanley over, if that is agreeable to the Court of
' Great Britain : if not, the King will keep a vessel, in the Port of Calais,
' which shall transport M. Bussy to England, in which case it will be proper to
' know what kind of vessel his Britannic Majesty will chuse to bring Mr. Stan-
' ley to Calais.

' I believe your Excellency will find these observations proper, and that you
' will send me your answer as soon as possible.

No. XIV.

Mr. Pitt's Answer to the Duke De Choiseul, of the 11th May, 1761.

' SIR,

' THE King my Master has learnt with real satisfaction, by the letter which
' your Excellency did me the honour to write of the 4th of this month,
' that the sentiments of the Most Christian King are conformable to those of
' his Majesty with respect to the mutual dispatch of the Ministers from the two
' Courts,

' I hope your Excellency will be persuaded, that I have a lively sense of the
' value of those obliging sentiments with which you have been pleased to honour
' me, and that, conscious as I am of your superior qualities, which have engaged
' the approbation of every Court, I perceive in its full extent how flattering a
' circumstance it would have been for me to have had the honour of treating per-
' sonally

'.fonally with your Excellency upon fo interefting an object, and to have fhared
'with you, in point of zeal for the profperous conduct of the Peace, the fa-
'tisfaction of co-operating more immediately to give the people affurance of
'the effects of the falutary difpofitions of the Kings our Mafters. I fhall never-
'thelefs take real pleafure, upon all occafions, to pay the refpect due to M. Buf-
'fy's character, as well as to his merit; and I can affure you, Sir, that the
'happinefs which that Minifter has had, of being ufed to transact bufinefs with
'your Excellency, is an additional circumftance which cannot but intereft me
'extremely in his behalf.

'I am perfuaded that Mr. Stanley, who is defcended from an illuftrious fami-
'ly, and who entertains noble fentiments, will ufe all his endeavours to merit
'the honour of your Excellency's efteem, and he wifhes to be recommended to
'your favour.

'You will fee, Sir, by my private letter, the reflections which have occurred
'in relation to the precautionary arrangements, which your Excellency propofed
'to fettle, and I hope that no farther impediments will remain on this fub-
'ject.

'I have the honour to be, &c.
'Signed W. Pitt."

No. XV.

Another Letter from Mr. Pitt to the D. de Choifeul, of the 11th May, 1761.

S I R,

'I Have received the three paffports, which your Excellency has done me the
'honour to tranfmit for Mr. Stanley, in quality of Minifter from the King my
'Mafter, and I in return tranfmit to you a fecond, which his Majefty has granted
'for the veffel which the Moft Chriftian King fhall think proper to order for
'tranfporting M. Buffy into England; and I annex the order to the Officers of
'the cuftoms, for the free importation of the effects and baggage of the faid Mi-
'nifter.

'As to what relates, Sir, to the obfervations which you thought yourfelf
'obliged to make, to warrant the execution of the commiffion of thofe two
'Minifters, it is with great fatisfaction I affure your Excellency, that the King,
'in conformity with the fentiments of his Moft Chriftian Majefty, is of
'opinion,

1. 'That the two Minifters fhould be charged with ample power from the
'Kings their Mafters, to make ufe of as occafion fhall offer.

2. 'That the two Minifters ought, each of them, to have Letters of Cre-
'dence from their Majefties, which they fhall not need to deliver but to the
'Secretaries of the refpective States, in the manner fpecified by your Excel-
'lency.

3. It,

3. ' It is the intention of his Majesty, that M. Bussy should absolutely en-
' joy in England, the same rights, prerogatives, franchises and liberties, as if
' the two Courts were in the midst of peace, and which Mr. Stanley, in pursu-
' ance of the intention of his Most Christian Majesty, is to enjoy in France;
' and that as to the dispatch of Couriers, as well as every thing else which con-
' cerns the two Ministers, the tenor of the third Article of . Observations relative
' to this head, shall be observed in every respect.

' As to what remains, concerning the time of the departure of the said Mi-
' nisters, as also concerning the manner of their crossing the sea, the King is of
' opinion, that in order to obviate all difficulties, Mr. Stanley and M. Bussy
' may respectively repair to Dover and Calais, to cross the sea each of them in
' a vessel appertaining to their own nation, which the Kings their Masters shall
' keep ready for that purpose in the two ports aforesaid. It is in confidence
' of this disposition, that I am obliged to acquaint your Excellency, that the
' King will dispatch Mr. Stanley from London, so that he may reach Dover on
' the 23d of this month, unless we learn that a time so near at hand should be
' inconvenient to the Court of France; and the King my Master relies, with full
' confidence, in M. Bussy's repairing to Calais on the aforesaid day, that the
' two Ministers may cross the sea without delay, as far as the circumstances of
' wind and navigation will permit them. I will add to your Excellency, that
' Mr. Stanley will make use of a packet-boat from Dover, and that M. Bussy
' may cross from Calais to England in whatever vessel his Most Christian Majesty
' shall judge convenient.

' I flatter myself that your Excellency will find that these arrangements will
' equally facilitate the method of the two Ministers repairing to their recipro-
' cal destinations without inconvenience.

' I have the honour to be, &c.
" Signed W. Pitt."

The Courts in alliance with France, without opposing this Negotiation with
the Court of London, expressed great uneasiness at the reciprocal dispatch of
the two Ministers: they were encouraged, however, by the promise which the
King made to them, of communicating with the utmost confidence, a detail of
the several objects which should be treated of, either at London or Versailles.
In the Declaration made to them on the part of the King, they at once admired
his Majesty's steadiness to his engagements, and that generosity with which he determined to sacrifice his personal interests, in order to come to a speedy and firm
reconciliation with England.

M. Bussy set out for London : his instructions were extremely simple : the basis of them regarded the proposition of *Uti Possidetis*, and he was enjoined,

1. To demand of the British Minister, whether the King of England accepted
of the periods annexed to the proposition of *Statu Quo*, and if his Britannic Majesty did not accept of them, What new periods he proposed to France ?

2. To declare to the Court of London, That the war which the King waged
against England, was entirely distinct from that of the Empress Queen against
the

the King of Pruſſia, and that conſequently, except as to Weſel and Gueldres, which appertained to her Imperial Majeſty, the King was at liberty to cauſe his forces to evacuate Gottingen, Heſſe, and the county of Hanau, but that his Majeſty made this evacuation to depend on two conditions: Firſt, That the Court of England ſhould give proper ſecurity, that the army commanded by Prince Ferdinand ſhould be diſbanded, and not ſerve againſt the King's Allies. Secondly, That his Britannic Majeſty would agree on ſome reſtitution which ſhould be judged reaſonable on the part of England, as a compenſation for the French troops evacuating Gottingen, the Landgraviate of Heſſe, and the county of Hanau.

Mr. Stanley arrived at Marly at the ſame time that Mr. Buſſy arrived at London. The Engliſh Miniſter, at the very firſt conference, declared in the name of his court, that the King his Maſter would ſupport his Allies with *Efficacy and good Faith* (Theſe were the terms he made uſe of.) The King's Miniſter who conferred with Mr. Stanley, anſwered him by a Declaration equally preciſe, with reſpect to his Majeſty's intention to fulfil his engagements with regard to the Allies of France: but as the Peace between the Empreſs Queen and the King of Pruſſia was to be negociated at the Congreſs at Augſbourg, which was fixed for the pacification of Germany, the D. de Choiſeul obſerved that the differences between her Imperial Majeſty and the King of Pruſſia were by no means the ſubject on which the French and Engliſh Miniſters were reciprocally diſpatched.

The ſubſequent conferences paſſed in diſcuſſing the periods fixed in the Memorial of the 26th March; but the Engliſh Miniſter, both at London and at Paris, eluded giving any poſitive anſwer on that ſubject.

It is neceſſary to obſerve, that the Britiſh Court had reſolved on the enterprize againſt Belleiſle, ſince the Memorial of the month of March. The expectation of ſucceſs from that Expedition, no doubt retarded, on their part, a categorical anſwer in relation to the epochs.

Mr. Pitt, being preſſed on that ſubject by M. Buſſy, had ſhewn himſelf averſe from declaring any thing deciſive; on which his Majeſty wrote to his Miniſter at London, to elucidate and fix preciſely the baſis of the Negociation, relative to the *Uti Poſſidetis* and the epochs, and by that means to accelerate the Negociation of peace. The iſland of Belleiſle was taken: Mr. Pitt then gave M. Buſſy the Memorial here annexed.

No. XVI.

The Memorial of the Britiſh Miniſter of the 17th June 1761.

'MR. Stanley having repreſented by his letter of the 8th of June, that the
' D. de Choiſeul, in the courſe of their conferences, had agreed *That the*
' *epochs muſt ſtill remain a matter of Negociation, but that his Excellency neverthelefs*
' *was of opinion, that in the preſent ſtate of that affair, according to the natural and*
' *uſual courſe of things, his Moſt Chriſtian Majeſty having already named the 1ſt of*
' *September, July, and May, his Britannic Majeſty ſhould proceed, either by accept-*
' *ing of thoſe days, or by naming others more agreeable to his intentions, which were*
' *probably regulated by preparations and deſigns of which the Court of France was ig-*
norant;

' norant ; *that this method appeared to him more likely to expedite the bufinefs than*
' *the making of re-iterated propofitions on their part, which could only be grounded*
' *on mere conjecture.* It is upon this footing, that, in order to make a return to
' the above invitation on the part of France, as well as in confequence of his
' Majefty's having accepted the propofition of the faid Court of the 26th March
' laft, his Majefty offers to agree with the Moft Chriftian King, that the firft day
' of July, September and November following, fhall refpectively be the diffe-
' rent periods or epochs, to fix the *Uti Poffidetis* which France has propofed to
' make the bafis of the treaty which may be negociated between the two Powers.
' All other conquefts made beyond thofe periods fhall be mutually reftored.
' But as his Majefty is of opinion that epochs which have no reference to the ac-
' tual fignature of fomething obligatory between the two Crowns, muft necef-
' farily be only a vain illufion, void of ufe or reality ; or that it might even hap-
' pen that in the end they may prove the fource of intricate difputes, and dan-
' gerous and captious altercations ; and the King having no other view but to
' concur with the upright intentions of his Moft Chriftian Majefty, in accelerat-
' ing and confirming the bleffing of peace to both nations, his Majefty only of-
' fers to agree to the aforefaid epoch, on the two following conditions :

' 1. That every thing which fhall be happily adjufted between the two Crowns,
' in relation to their particular war, fhall be made obligatory, final, and conclu-
' five, independent of the fate of the Negociation at Augfbourg, which is to com-
' pofe and terminate the difputes of Germany, and to re-eftablifh a general
' peace.

' 2. That the faid definitive Treaty of Peace between Great Britain and France
' fhall be concluded, figned and ratified, or preliminary articles to that end, be-
' tween this and the firft of Auguft next.

' The Reftitution of the prizes taken at fea, fhall be regulated according to
' the refpective terms which are ufual for different parts of the globe; which
' terms are to be computed from the day of the fignature of the faid definitive
' treaty, or of preliminary articles of peace, in cafe a ratification enfues.

' The King defiring farther to facilitate the falutary work of Peace, as far as
' reafon and juftice will admit, declares moreover, that with regard to Belleifle,
' his Majefty will agree, in the faid future Treaty, to enter into compenfation for
' that important conqueft.

' With regard to farther compenfations for any part of the other conquefts
' made by the Crown of Great Britain, his Majefty referves himfelf, till he fhall
' learn what are the Moft Chriftian King's defires in that refpect, which when
' he fhall know, his Majefty will open himfelf with perfect fincerity and good
' faith.'

We fee by this Memorial, the epochs which England required to determine the
Uti poffidetis, were farther diftant by two months than thofe offered by France ;
and it was evident that as the enterprize againft Belleifle had determined Eng'and
to defer her anfwer with regard to the epochs, fo the fuccefs of that expedition
had made them refolve to fix the term of July for Europe, fpecified in the

Englifh

English Memorial, instead of May, which was proposed by the French Memorial.

England made the epochs she assigned depend on two conditions. The first of those conditions departed both from the letter and the spirit of the Memorial of the 26th of March: for although France had proposed to treat of a peace separately with England; nevertheless his Majesty's intention was not regulated by this principle of the negotiation, that peace could be concluded with England, without providing for the peace of Germany. In fact, the Memorial of the 26th March, from which the Court of England drew such advantageous arguments, opened with this expression, *The Most Christian King is desirous that the particular peace of France with England should be united with the general peace of Europe.*

The second condition, with respect to discussing and settling the Articles, so that they might be signed and ratified by the 1st of August, was very difficult to be fulfilled in regard to a War, which extended over the four quarters of the globe, this condition proposed by England not being known to France till the end of June.

France returned no specific answer to the Memorial of the Court of London ; but verbally acquiesced, as far as possible, to the second condition : and with regard to the first, the King required the consent of the Court of Vienna, to conclude a separate peace with England. This Consent was necessary, since, from the beginning, as is before mentioned, it was agreed between her Majesty and his allies, that they should treat of peace separately ; but that all the belligerant parties should come to a conclusion together.

Though the Empress Queen was perfectly sensible of the prejudice which the alliance might sustain by a negociation in Germany, at a time that France was at peace with England ; yet her Imperial Majesty, to oblige the King, agreed, on this occasion, to sacrifice her own interest to the desire which his Majesty expressed for the establishment of peace. This princess consented to the separate accommodation of France with England, upon this express and equitable condition, that nothing should be therein stipulated, ...ich might be contrary to the interest of the House of Austria.

The conclusion of the British Memorial contained a Proposition for France to make some overtures with regard to the compensations. The King availed himself of this intimation, and ordered a Memorial to be prepared, including specific propositions, which put the negociation in a proper train, and fixed its basis on express and determinate points.

France was perfectly sensible how disadvantageous it was to her, to make her enemies acquainted with the favourable conditions which it was agreed to allow them, in order to succeed in the re establishment of peace : she was conscious, that it was just and reasonable for France, who made the first proposition of *Uti possidetis*, to wait till England explained herself concerning the Compensations : but she flattered herself, that England was sincerely desirous of re-establishing the union between the two Crowns ; and the advantages, which would redound to England from the offers of France, were so visible and extensive, that there was no suspicion that the Court of London would increase the difficulties of a nego-

D   ciation

ciation, which France was zealous to terminate without delay, and to the fatif-faction of the two powers.

Before a Memorial of propofitions was fent in form to the court of London, his Majefty's Minifter, entrufted to confer with M. Stanley, gave him previous affurances of the facrifices which his Majefty had refolved to make. He autho-rized him to write word, that France would guaranty the poffeffion of Canada to England, provided that England would reftore to the King the ifland of Cape Breton, and confirm the right of the French to fifh, and dry their fifh, in the gulf of St. Lawrence, upon the coaft, and in the ifland, of Newfoundland. As the ifland of Cape Breton, if fortified, might afford England matter of jealoufy, the French Minifter told M. Stanley, that the King engaged to deftroy all the fortifications which might remain in that ifland, and not to erect any new ones upon any pretence whatever. The port of Louifbourg being to be confidered only as a fhelter for the fifhermen in the gulf of St. Laurence, and on the coaft of Newfoundland, France offered to reftore the ifland of Minorca to England, pro-vided they would give up the iflands of Guadaloupe and Marigalante in return.

With regard to the Eaft Indies, they propofed that the treaty of the Sieurs Godeheu and Saunders, made in the year 1755, fhou'd be confirmed. That treaty, although advantageous to the Englifh Company, was judged to be moft effectual for maintaining peace between the two Companies, and to recal them to views of commerce much more analogous to their reciprocal interefts, than profpects of conquefts, which had hitherto kept them at variance.

With refpect to Africa, France required that England fhould reftore either Senegal or Goree, and on thofe conditions the King declared that he would eva-cuate Gottingen, Heffe, and the county of Hanau, would withdraw his forces upon the Rhine and the Maine, and would leave no French troops in Germany but in proportion to what troops of the enemy remained affembled in the Britifh army at Weftphalia.

Mr. Stanley took notes of thefe overtures which were made by the D. de Choifeul, who told him moreover that the propofitions made to the Englifh Minifter, could only be confidered as intimations of conditions which might pof-fibly be agreed to, and as preliminary fteps to the Memorial which France deter-mined to tranfmit to the Court of London in form, if the points difcuffed in the conference of the D. de Choifeul with Mr. Stanley fhould be thought proper to ferve as a bafis for the Negotiation of peace.

The anfwer from England arrived the 30th June. Mr. Stanley had a con-ference with the D. de Choifeul refpecting this anfwer; and in the courfe of that conference, he ftarted three difficulties on the part of his Court. The firft con-cerned Cape Breton. England abfolutely refufed to cede that ifland to France, even upon the condition, that no military eftablifhment whatever fhould be kept on foot there. Mr. Stanley intimated that his Court had no intention of reftoring any ifland or port in the Gulf of St. Laurence, or within reach of that Gulf. He added, that England would make no difficulty of allowing the li-berty of fifhing and drying the fifh on the fhores and coafts of Newfoundland; but

but that this would be granted on condition that Dunkirk was demolifhed, as it was ftipulated to have been by the treaty of Utrecht.

Till this moment, no mention had been made of Dunkirk, either in what had paffed by word of mouth, or in writing, with relation to the peace between the two Crowns.

In fact, it was unjuft to infift on this article, fince the Court of London, having had this principle eftablifhed, in treating of peace, to adhere to the Memorial of *Uti poffedetis* of the 26th March, they could not pretend that the prefent ftate of Dunkirk was comprized in the *Uti poffidetis* of France.

The liberty of fifhing, and the fhelter without fortifications, was the compenfation for the ceffion of all Canada, and of the guaranty which France offered to make to England of that confiderable part of North America. The reftitution of the ifland of Minorca was certainly equivalent to the ceffion of Guadaloupe and Marigalante; and the evacuation of Heffe and the other countries appertaining to the Elector of Hanover and to the Landgrave, was compenfated by the reftitution of Senegal and Goree, and of Belle-Ifle, which had been conquered fince the Memorial of the 26th March, and after the propofition of the epochs propofed in that Memorial.

Befides, France had declared, at the time of taking Belle-Ifle, that fhe did not underftand that conqueft was to have been an object of compenfation, and that fhe thought the keeping of Belle-Ifle would be more expenfive than profitable to England.

Mr. Stanley, in oppofing the ceffion of Ifle Royal to France, abfolutely refufed the reftitution of Senegal and Goree, pretending that Senegal could not be fecurely maintained without Goree; in the end, he infifted on the demolition of Dunkirk as a condition abfolutely neceffary. The article relating to Germany was not negotiated on his part; and after feveral conferences it was agreed that France fhould prepare a Memorial of fpecific propofitions, which fhould be fent to England. The Memorial was drawn, and is here annexed.

No. XVII.

The French Memorial, 15th *July,* 1761.

' THE Negotiations of peace entered upon between France and England,
' have proved that the Sovereigns fincerely wifh to re-eftablifh that union
' and amity, fo agreeable to humanity, between the two Crowns; and the refo-
' lution in which the King concurs, in conjunction with his Britannic Majefty,
' to terminate by a precife and durable treaty, the differences which have oc-
' cafioned the prefent war, has determined his Majefty, always maintaining the
' fpirit and letter of the declaration of the 26th March laft, in relation to the
' means of procuring peace, to explain more precifely by this Memorial, the
' conditions which appear to him moft proper to accomplifh the defirable end
' which influences him as well as the King of England.

' But the King declares at the fame time, that he entrufts this propofition
' with the King of Great Britain, that if it fhould not be accepted by his Bri-

' tan-

' tannic Majefty, or fhould not ferve as a Bafis for the Negotiation of the future
' peace, the Court of London fhall in no circumftances take advantage of it,
' the faid propofition made in confidence to the King of Great Britain having
' no other object than the accelerating of a Negotiation in which the two Crowns
' are fo much interefted.

' The *Uti poffidetis* expreffed in the declaration of the 26th March, is adopted
' on both fides; it would be difficult for either party to reject it; for though it
' was not expreffed, it is properly according to what they poffefs only either law-
' fully or by conqueft, that the parties can negotiate together concerning peace,
' and the compenfations requifite for that purpofe.

' The periods of the *Statu Quo*, which form the fecond effential article in the
' declaration of the 26th March, and which have remained in Negotiation be-
' tween the two Courts, have not yet been fettled. The Court of France has
' propofed the epochs of May, July and September; that of England has pro-
' pofed the epochs of July, September and November. That queftion will be
' determined without farther Negotiation, if the fcheme of the following treaty
' is adopted by the Court of London, for then all the epochs will be valid, as
' that of the peace will unite the fentiments and opinions of the two Kings.
' It is the compenfations therefore which will determine the epochs and the
' peace, and it is to fettle them that his Majefty propofes the following articles
' to the King of Great Britain.

Article I.

' The King cedes and guaranties Canada to the King of England, fuch as
' it has been and in right ought to be poffeffed by France, without reftriction,
' and without the liberty of returning upon any pretence whatever againft this
' ceffion and guaranty, and without interrupting the crown of England in the
' entire poffeffion of Canada.

II.

' The King, in making over his full right of fovereignty over Canada to the
' King of England, annexes four conditions to the ceffion. Firft, that the free
' exercife of the Roman Catholic religion fhall be maintained there, and that
' the King of England will give the moft precife and effectual orders that his
' new Roman Catholic fubjects may, as heretofore, make public profeffion of
' their religion, according to the rites of the Roman Church.
' Secondly, that the French inhabitants or others, who have been fubjects of
' the King in Canada, may retire into the French colonies with all poffible free-
' dom and fecurity; that they may be allowed to fell their effects, and to tranf-
' port their property as well as their perfons, without being reftrained in their
' emigration, on any pretence whatever (except for debt;) and the Englifh go-
' vernment fhall engage to procure them the means of tranfportation at as little
' expence as poffible.

' Thirdly,

'Thirdly, that the limits of Canada, with regard to Louisiana, shall be clearly
'and firmly established, as well as those of Louisiana and Virginia, in such man-
'ner, that after the execution of peace, there may be no more difficulties between
'the two nations, with respect to the construction of the limits with regard to
'Louisiana, whether with respect to Canada, or the other possessions of England.
N. B. M. Bussy has a Memorial on the subject of the limits of Louisiana,
which gives him power to come to a final treaty on that article with the
Ministry of his Britannic Majesty.

'Fourthly, that the liberty of fishing, and of drying their cod-fish on the banks of
'Newfoundland, may be confirmed to the French as heretofore : and as this con-
'firmation would be illusory, if the French vessels had not a shelter in those parts
'appertaining to their nation, the King of Great Britain, in consideration of the
'guaranty of his new conquests, shall restore Isle Royal, or Cape Breton, to be
'enjoyed by France in entire sovereignty. It is agreed, to fix a value on this
'restitution, that France shall not, under any denomination whatever, erect any
'fortifications on the island, and shall confine herself to maintain civil establish-
'ments there, and the port for the convenience of the fishing vessels landing there.

III.

'France shall restore to England the island of Minorca, and Fort St. Phi-
'lip, in the same condition it was in when it was conquered by the King's forces,
'together with the artillery belonging to England, which was in the fort at the
'time of taking the island.

IV.

'In consideration of this restitution, England, in her turn, shall restore to
'France the island of Guadaloupe and Marigalante; and those two islands shall
'be ceded in the same condition they were in at the time they were conquered by
'the arms of England.

V.

'The islands called neuter, are Dominica, Saint Vincent, Saint Lucia, and
'Tabago. The two first are occupied by the Carribees, under the protection of
'France, according to the treaty of 1660 : they shall remain in the condition
'they have been since that treaty.

'The Crown of England has not yet shewn any title, which gives them a right
'over the two last; nevertheless, it shall be a matter of negociation between the
'two crowns, either that the four islands shall remain absolutely neuter, or that
'the two possessed by the Carribees alone shall be declared neuter; and that Eng-
'land shall enter into possession, as sovereign, over the island of Tabago, in the
'same manner as France over that of St. Lucia, saving, at all times, the right
'of a third person, with whom the two crowns will explain themselves, if such a
'right exists.

VI.

VI.

‘ It would be advantageous for the companies of the two nations in the
‘ Eaſt-Indies, to abſtain for ever from all military views and conqueſts, to re-
‘ ſtrain themſelves, and mutually to aſſiſt each other in the buſineſs of commerce,
‘ which more properly belongs to them. The preciſe ſituation in which the two na-
‘ tions ſtand, is not known in France : wherefore the King, in order to confine
‘ himſelf, in that reſpect, to the object moſt uſeful, both for the preſent and
‘ hereafter, to the two companies, propoſes to the King of England the treaty
‘ concluded between the Sieurs Godeheu and Saunders, as a baſis for the re-eſta-
‘ bliſhment of the peace of Aſia.

VII.

‘ The colonies of South America, in poſſeſſion of the French, neceſſarily require
‘ negroes to cultivate them ; the French ſettlements of Senegal and Goree ſupplied
‘ the wants of the French colonies in this reſpect. England, in keeping thoſe ſet-
‘ tlements, would prejudice France, without procuring any poſitive advantages
‘ for herſelf ; and the union which the two Sovereigns ſo ſincerely wiſh to eſta-
‘ bliſh between the two Crowns, leaves no room to ſuppoſe that the Court of
‘ London has any ſuch intentions of miſchief. Nevertheleſs, France, with a view
‘ to the bleſſings of peace, offers England the choice of the poſſeſſions of Sene-
‘ gal or Goree, meaning that one or the other poſſeſſion ſhall be reſtored and
‘ guarantied to the King by his Britannic Majeſty.

VIII.

‘ The Iſland of Belle-Iſle and the fortreſs conquered by the arms of England
‘ ſhall be reſtored to France, together with the artillery therein at the time of the
‘ conqueſt.

IX.

‘ In conſideration of the 8th Article to be granted by England, the King
‘ will cauſe his forces in Germany to evacuate the Landgraviate of Heſſe,
‘ the county of Hanau, as well as the town, which ſhall not be occupied by the
‘ troops of either Power, leaving the navigation of the Maine free, and thoſe
‘ parts of the Electorate of Hanover occupied by the French troops; and theſe
‘ evacuations ſhall be preceded by a ſuſpenſion of arms between the two Crowns,
‘ which ſuſpenſion of arms ſhall take place from the day of the ratification of
‘ the preliminaries, or the Article of the Definitive Treaty, not only in Germa-
‘ ny, but in all parts of the world where France and England are at war.

X.

‘ As the King is under an engagement with the Empreſs Queen, to ſtipulate
‘ nothing in his Treaty of Peace with England which may be diſadvantageous
‘ to her Imperial Majeſty, and as it was foreſeen that, in caſe of a ſuſpenſion be-
‘ tween the French and Britiſh forces, the German troops in the pay of Eng-
‘ land might join thoſe of the King of Pruſſia againſt the Auſtrian armies,
‘ the King, faithful to his engagements with his allies, and very far from in-
‘ tending to ſettle any thing to her prejudice, propoſes to the King of England,
‘ that

' that it may be agreed between them, that his Britannic Majeſt will undertake
' that no part of the forces which compoſe Prince Ferdinand's army, ſhall,
' under any pretence whatever, or under any denomination, join the army of
' his Pruſſian Majeſty, or act offenſively againſt the Empreſs Queen or her allies;
' and in like manner, no French forces, under any pretence, ſhall join the Im-
' perial army, or ſerve againſt the Allies of Great Britain. To aſcertain theſe
' poſitions, it ſhall be farther concluded, that after theſe evacuations, the army
' of the Upper Rhine, commanded by Marſhal Broglio, ſhall retire towards the
' Maine, the Necker and the Rhine, occupying Francfort; and that of the
' Lower Rhine commanded by Marſhal Soubiſe, ſhall, on the other ſide, retired
' towards the Rhine, occupying Weſel and Guelders.

' The countries belonging to the King of Pruſſia, on the Lower Rhine, have
' been conquered, and are actually governed in the name of the Empreſs Queen:
' the King would not undertake to evacuate them without the conſent of her Im-
' perial Majeſty, and before the ſucceſs of the Negotiations at the Congreſs at
' Augſbourg, which is to reſtore Peace between the Empreſs and the King of
' Pruſſia; but as it would be diſadvantageous to the two Crowns to maintain a
' conſiderable body of national forces in Germany, which, in time of peace,
' would remain in abſolute inactivity, and, by the Conventions of the Treaty,
' would become uſeleſs in every reſpect to the Allies of France and England, the
' King undertakes, that, from the time that his Britannic Majeſty do recal the
' Engliſh whom he has ſent to his army in Germany, he will cauſe double the
' number of French forces in his Majeſty's armies on the Upper and Lower
' Rhine to return to France, ſo that no French troops ſhall continue in thoſe parts,
' but in proportion to thoſe which the King of England ſhall keep in pay.

XI.

' If before the execution of the Treaty, one of the two Powers ſhould make
' any conqueſts, in whatever part of the world it be, they ſhall be reſtored
' without heſitation, and without requiring any recompence.

XII.

' The captures made at ſea by England before the declaration of the war,
' are objects of legal reſtitution, and which the King will willingly ſubmit to the
' juſtice of the King of England and the Engliſh tribunals; in fact, ſubjects,
' who under the faith of treaties, the law of nations, and in time of peace, fol-
' low their trade and navigation, cannot with juſtice become ſufferers by the
' miſunderſtandings ſubſiſting in the cabinets of the two Courts, before they have
' any intimation of it. Declarations of war are eſtabliſhed by the law of nations,
' for no other purpoſe, but to make public to the people the conteſts between
' their Sovereigns, and to give them warning, that their perſons and fortunes
' are, in danger from an enemy. Unleſs ſuch declaration is agreed upon, there
' can be no public ſecurity; every individual would be in danger, or in fear,
' every moment that he ſtepped beyond the limits of his own country. If theſe
' principles are inconteſtible, nothing remains but to examine the date of the de-
' claration

'claration of war, between the two Crowns, and the date of the Captures; all
'that has been taken prior to the declaration, cannot be adjudged lawful prize,
'without overthrowing the moſt ſalutary laws; it will be in vain to alledge that
'the French began hoſtilities, and that the captures were taken by way of re-
'prizal. What connection can there be between ſuppoſed hoſtilities offered at
'Fort Duqueſne, and the capture of trading veſſels in the ſouth part of Ame-
'rica? Theſe hoſtilities are the motives for the Declaration of War; but the ef-
'fects of that Declaration cannot take place, till after the ſaid Declaration is
'made public; and it would be unjuſt to make individuals ſuſtain a loſs, who
'are totally ignorant of the facts and circumſtances of a latent hoſtility in a
'corner of the world, which has occaſioned a general war between the two
'nations.

'This argument is deemed unanſwerable in France; and it is on this footing
'that the King challenges the right of nations, to the end that ſome expedient
'may be agreed upon in the future Treaty as a recompenſe for the captures made
'upon his ſubjects previous to the Declaration of War, without entering into any
'diſcuſſion about Reprizals, which ſhould be forgotten when the two Courts
'draw near to an agreement. France conſults nothing but the intereſt of the in-
'dividuals who have been ſufferers, and does not pretend to include the King's
'ſhips taken before the Declaration in the ſettlement of the Captures, as the loſs
'of the King's ſhips may be conſidered as a conſequence of the motives of the
'War.

XIII.

'Though, during the courſe of the preſent War, the article of former Trea-
'ties which guaranty the ſucceſſion to the Throne of Great Britain, according to
'the preſent eſtabliſhment, has not been infringed, neverthéleſs the King is
'well diſpoſed to comprize that Guaranty in the future Treaty, if the King of
'England deſires it.

XIV.

'The priſoners made on each ſide, as well by ſea as land, ſhall be ſet at li-
'berty, and ſent home without ranſom, immediately on the ratification of the
'Peace.

'His Britannic Majeſty will readily perceive, that theſe articles are not drawn in
'the form of a treaty; they are only offered to him as articles explained in their
'full extent, which elucidate the ſentiments of France, and put the two Crowns
'in a condition to treat upon certain and diſtinct objects.'

This Memorial was ſent to London on the 15th of July. The date is mentioned, becauſe the Britiſh Miniſtry reproached the French Miniſtry with having
delayed the diſpatch of the Memorial; and it is proper to obſerve, that the laſt
anſwer from England did not reach France till the 1ſt of July; that there was a
neceſſity of having ſeveral conferences with Mr. Stanley, to form the ſcheme of a
treaty, which comprehended the preciſe diſcuſſion of objects in every part of the
world where the two Crowns are at war, and which was to produce the re-eſta-

5   bliſhment

blifhment of peace, or the continuance of the war. The reproach of a delay of fifteen days, upon fo interefting a bufinefs, was certainly an inftance of injuftice.

However that point be fettled, it is fubmitted to the difcernment and juftice of all Europe to determine, whether the Memorial of France of the 15th July did not confirm the principles of reconciliation, which had hitherto appeared in every ftep taken by that Crown. The Court of France acted with fuch integrity, in the confidence fhe repofed in the pacific difpofition of England, that having facrificed confiderable interefts, fhe carried her forecaft fo far, as to intimate to the Court of London her apprehenfions left the matters which remained to be difcuffed between Spain and England, and which were not yet adjufted, fhould in the end prove an obftacle to the duration and folidity of the peace which the King and his Britannic Majefty were defirous of re-eftablifhing between them.

In confequence of thefe apprehenfions, M. Buffy had orders to remind the Court of London, with refpect to the fubject of the Neutral Iflands, fpecified in the 20th article of the Memorial, that his Catholic Majefty made fome claims upon thofe Iflands, with which the Court of Madrid had recently made that of Verfailles acquainted. The French Minifter was charged at the fame time to reprefent to Mr. Pitt, how dangerous it would be to determine the fate of thofe Iflands, without paying regard to the claims of his Catholic Majefty. M. Buffy was ordered to add, that it was evident that the Court of Spain would agree to the fettlement which fhould be made between France and England, in relation to the four Iflands in queftion, provided that the three articles negotiated at London on the part of the Court of Madrid, were adjufted at the fame time that the Peace with France fhould be concluded there; and to teftify a fincerity as laudable as it was perfect, M. Buffy was charged to annex to the Memorial of Propofitions, the particular Memorial which follows relative to Spain.

No. XVIII.

The private Memorial of France, of 15th July, 1761, relating to Spain.

' AS it is effential, and agreeable to the defire of France and England, that the
' projected Treaty of Peace fhould ferve as a bafis for a folid reconciliation
' between the two Crowns, which may not be liable to be interrupted by the in-
' terefts of a third Power, and the engagements which either one or the other
' may have entered into previous to their reconciliation, he propofes that the
' King of Spain fhall be invited to guaranty the future Treaty of Peace between
' his Majefty and the King of Great Britain. This Guaranty will obviate all
' prefent and future inconveniences with regard to the folidity of the Peace.

' The King will not difguife from his Majefty, that the differences of Spain
' with England fill him with apprehenfions, and give him room to fear, that, if
' they are not adjufted, they will occafion a frefh war in Europe and America.
' The King of Spain has communicated to his Majefty the three articles which
' remain to be difcuffed between his Crown and the Crown of Britain: which
' are,

E   1. ' The

1. ' The reſtitution of ſome captures which have been made during the preſent
' war upon the Spaniſh Flag.

2. ' The privilege for the Spaniſh nation to fiſh upon the Banks of New-
' foundland.

3. ' The demolition of the Engliſh ſettlements made upon the Spaniſh territo-
' ries in the Bay of Honduras.

' Theſe three articles may be eaſily adjuſted agreeable to the equity of the two
' nations ; and the King earneſtly wiſhes, that ſome accommodations may be
' thought on, to the ſatisfaction of the Spaniſh and Engliſh nations, with regard
' to theſe articles ; but he cannot diſguiſe from England the danger he appre-
' hends, and of which he muſt neceſſarily partake, if theſe objects, which ſeem
' nearly to concern his Catholic Majeſty, ſhould be the occaſion of a War.   His
' Majeſty, therefore, deems it a principal point of conſideration in concluding a
' firm and advantageous Peace, that, at the ſame time that that deſirable Point
' ſhall be concluded between France and England, his Britannic Majeſty ſhould
' terminate his differences with Spain, and agree to invite his Catholic Majeſty
' to guaranty the Treaty which is to reconcile (pray Heaven for ever) his Ma-
' jeſty and the King of England.

' As to what remains, his Majeſty does not intimate his apprehenſion in this
' reſpect to the Court of London, but with the moſt ſincere and upright inten-
' tions to obviate every impediment which may ariſe hereafter to diſturb the
' union of the French and Engliſh nations ; and he deſires his Britannic Majeſty,
' whom he ſuppoſes influenced by the ſame good wiſhes, freely to communicate
' his ſentiments on ſo eſſential an object.'

The precaution of France to enſure the ſolidity of the Peace, comprized every
object which could conduce to that end.   The ſuccours which his Majeſty and
the King of England afforded their Allies in Germany, left a ſource of war ſtill
ſubſiſting, and an expence detrimental to both nations.   The King judged, that
the moſt natural means to put an end to the diſputes which the ſuccours to be afforded their reſpective Allies might produce, would be to come to an agreement
between France and England, that France, on her part, ſhould not yield any
kind of ſuccour to the Empreſs-Queen, and in like manner, that England
ſhould be bound not to furniſh any aſſiſtance to the King of Pruſſia.   It would
have been a violation of good faith to have ſtipulated this withdrawing of all ſuccour, without the conſent of the Allies.   The King required the conſent of the
Empreſs Queen, and obtained it early enough, for M. Buſſy to tranſmit the
following note to the Britiſh Miniſter relative to that object, at the ſame time
that he gave him the Memorial of the French propoſitions, and that which
related to Spain.

No.

No. XIX.

M. Buffy's Note to Mr. Pitt.

' SINCE the Memorial of the propofitions from France was formed, and at
' the inftant that the courier was ready to fet out for London, the King re-
' ceived the confent of the Emprefs Queen to a feparate peace with England,
' but upon two conditions :

1. ' To keep poffeffion of the countries belonging to the King of Pruffia.

2. ' That it fhall be ftipulated, that the King of Great Britain, neither in
' his capacity of King or Elector, fhall afford any fuccour, either in troops, or of
' any kind whatever, to the King of Pruffia ; and that his Britannic Majefty will
' undertake that the Hanoverian, Heffian, Brunfwickian, and the other Auxili-
' aries in alliance with Hanover, fhall not join the forces of the King of Pruffia,
' in like manner as France fhall engage, on her part, not to yield fuccour of any
' kind to the Emprefs Queen, nor her Allies.

' Both thefe conditions appear fo natural and equitable in themfelves, that
' his Majefty could not do otherwife than acquiefce in them, and he hopes that
' the King of Great Britain will be ready to adopt them.'

Upon reading thefe vouchers with attention, it may be obferved, that the Memorial containing the propofitions, clearly explains the means of reconciling
France and England with refpect to their particular interefts ; and that the Note,
No. XIX, removes all obftacles which the fuccours to be given to the Allies in Germany might throw in the way of a reconciliation between the two Crowns. In
fact, what could be more juft and advantageous both to France and England, in
the circumftances in which they ftood, than wholly and abfolutely to withdraw
from the war in Germany. Laftly, in order to prevent the flames of war from
breaking out afrefh in Europe, which the complaints of Spain might re-kindle,
and in which France, fooner or later, would have been forced to have taken
part ; nothing could be deemed more difcreet than the propofition contained in
the Memorial, No. XVIII. more efpecially as that propofition was the natural
refult of the good offices which his Catholic Majefty had offered to the Crown,
the preceding years, in order to mediate peace between them, which kind offices
had been accepted on the part of France by an authentic declaration, which had
not then been oppofed by England.

M. Buffy laid thefe feveral pieces before Mr. Pitt on the 23d of July. They
had been previoufly communicated to Mr. Stanley, to the end that that Minifter
might tranfmit a circumftantial account of them to his court, and that the Englifh Minifter might be apprized of the objects included in the difpatch, and
might be able to confer with M. Buffy thereupon without lofs of time. The
King had even tranfmitted very minute inftructions to his Minifter at London,
which contained frefh expedients for reconciling the differences of France with
England, in relation to the refpective poffeffions of the two Crowns in America,

Africa,

Africa, and Afia. His Majefty had forefeen that the taking of Pondicherry, of which an account came but a few days before, might occafion fome alteration which it might be neceffary to obviate by frefh facrifices, if fuch fhould be deemed expedient ; but the Englifh Minifter, in the conference at which the pieces were laid before him, difcovered his perfonal oppofition to peace : he refufed to agree to any of the articles in the Memorial of propofitions ; he entered very little into the particular motives of his oppofition ; he expatiated with fome warmth on the Memorial which related to Spain ; rejected the Note which concerned the Allies in Germany with difdain ; and concluded with faying, That he would take the directions of the King his Mafter, with refpect to thofe two laft pieces, and that he would tranfmit to Mr. Stanley the anfwer of his Britannic Majefty to the propofitions of France. In confequence of this, Mr. Pitt, having returned M. Buffy the Memorials concerning Spain and Germany, wrote a letter to him on the 24th of July, conceived in the following terms.

No. XX.

Mr. Pitt's Letter to M. Buffy, 24th July 1761.

SIR,

‘ HAVING explained myfelf, in our conference yefterday, with refpect to
‘ certain engagements of France with Spain, relative to the difputes of the
‘ latter Crown with Great Britain, of which your court never informed us, but at
‘ the very inftant of making, as fhe has done, her firft propofitions for the fe-
‘ parate peace of the two Crowns ; and as you have defired, for the fake of
‘ greater punctuality, to take a note of what paffed between us upon fo weighty
‘ a fubject, I here repeat, Sir, by his Majefty's order, the fame Declaration,
‘ word for word, which I made to you yefterday, and again anticipate you with
‘ refpect to the moft fincere fentiments of friendfhip and real regard on the part
‘ of his Majefty towards the Catholic King, in every particular confiftent with
‘ reafon and juftice. It is my duty to declare farther to you in plain terms, in
‘ the name of his Majefty, That he will not fuffer the difputes with Spain to be
‘ blended, in any manner whatever, in the Negotiation of Peace between the two
‘ Crowns ; to which I muft add, That it will be confidered as an affront to his
‘ Majefty's dignity, and as a thing incompatible with the fincerity of the Nego-
‘ tiation, to make farther mention of fuch a circumftance.

‘ Moreover, it is expected that France will not, at any time, prefume a right
‘ of intermeddling in fuch Difputes between Great Britain and Spain.

‘ Thefe Confiderations, fo juft and indifpenfible, have determined his Majefty
‘ to order me to return you the Memorial which occafions this, as wholly inad-
‘ miffible.

‘ I likewife return you, Sir, as totally inadmiffible, the Memorial relative to
‘ the King of Pruffia, as implying an Attempt upon the Honour of Great Bri-
‘ tain, and the Fidelity with which his Majefty will always fulfil his Engage-
‘ ments with his Allies.

‘ I have the Honour to be, &c.’

Signed Pitt.

The

The ſtyle of this Letter, and the manner of returning the Memorials, do not bear the marks of that conciliating temper, by which the Court of England would hitherto have been thought to have been influenced.

The Anſwers to the Memorial of the French Propoſitions, which were remitted to Verſailles on the 29th July, are extremely analogous with Mr. Pitt's Letter; they are dictated with an air of haughtineſs and deſpotiſm which might have ſhocked a Court of leſs conſequence than that of France. They follow word for word.

No. XXI.

The Anſwer of the Britiſh Court to the Memorial of French Propoſitions. 29th July, 1761.

A Paper of Articles to be delivered to Mr. Stanley, as the definitive propoſitions from the Court of Great Britain.

1. ' HIS Britannic Majeſty will never recede from the entire and total ceſſion on the Part of France, without any new limits, or any exception whatever, of all Canada and its appurtenances; and his Majeſty will never relax, with regard to the full and compleat ceſſion on the Part of France, of the Iſle of Cape Breton, and of all the other Iſlands in the Gulph or in the River of St Lawrence, with the right of fiſhing, which is inſeparably incident to the poſſeſſion of the aforeſaid Coaſts, and of the Canals or Streights which lead to them.

2. ' With reſpect to fixing the limits of Louiſiana, with regard to Canada, or the Engliſh Poſſeſſions ſituate on the Ohio, as alſo on the Coaſt of Virginia, it can never be allowed that whatever does not belong to Canada ſhall appertain to Louiſiana, nor that the boundaries of the laſt Province ſhould extend to Virginia, or to the Britiſh poſſeſſions on the borders of the Ohio; the nations and countries which lie intermediate, and which form the true barrier between the aforeſaid provinces, not being proper, on any account, to be directly or by neceſſary conſequence ceded to France, even admitting them to be included in the limits of Louiſiana.

3. ' Senegal, with all its Rights and Dependancies upon the River which bears its name, ſhall be ceded to Great Britain in the moſt full and ample manner; as alſo the Iſland of Goree, ſo eſſentially connected with Senegal.

4. ' Dunkirk ſhall be reduced to the condition in which it ought to have been after the Treaty of Utrecht, without which no Peace can be concluded; and upon that condition only can his Majeſty ever conſent to enter on the conſideration of the demand which France has made, viz. The reſtitution of the privilege granted by the thirteenth article of the ſaid treaty, with certain limitations and under certain reſtrictions, for the ſubjects of France to fiſh and dry their fiſh on part of the Banks of Newfoundland.

5. ' Though the titles by which the Kingdom of Great Britain has, on many occaſions, maintained its right to the Iſlands of St. Lucia and Tabago, have never yet been refuted; and though his Majeſty by force of arms has acquired

poſſeſſion

'poffeffion of St. Dominica, and of the French Colony eftablifhed before the
'commencement of the war; neverthelefs his Majefty, from that principle of
'moderation, which is fo becoming to Kings, will confent to an equal partition
'of the four Iflands, commonly called the Neutral Iflands, which partition fhall
'be regulated in the enfuing treaty.

6. 'The ifland of Minorca fhall be immediately reftored in the condition it
'was at the time of its being taken, together with the artillery, &c. appertain-
'ing to that ifland.

7. 'France fhall immediately reftore and evacuate the conquefts fhe has made
'over his Majefty's Allies in Germany; that is to fay, of all the States and
'Countries appertaining to the Landgrave of Heffe, to the Duke of Brunfwic,
'and to the Electorate of Hanover, as alfo of Wefel, and of all the places and
'territories belonging to the King of Pruffia, in poffeffion of the arms of France.
'In a word, France fhall make a general evacuation of all her conquefts, on the
'fide of Heffe, Weftphalia, and its countries.

8. 'The King of Great Britain on his part, agrees to furrender to his Moft
'Chriftian Majefty, 1. The important conqueft of Belle-Ifle. 2. His Majefty
'likewife confents to furrender to the Moft Chriftian King the opulent ifland
'of Guadaloupe, with that of Marigalante.

9. 'The treaty concluded between Meffrs. Saunders and Godeheu, cannot
'be admitted as the bafis of the re-eftablifhment of the peace in Afia, becaufe
'that provifional treaty has had no confequences, and becaufe thofe provifions
'are by no means applicable to the prefent ftate of affairs in the Indies, by the
'final reduction of the poffeffions and fettlements of the French company in the
'Eaft Indies; but as the perfect and final fettlement with regard to that coun-
'try can only be made in conformity to certain rights abfolutely appertaining
'to the Englifh company, and as the King cannot juftly difpofe of their rights
'without their confent, it muft neceffarily be left to the Companies of the two
'nations to adjuft the terms of accommodation and reconciliation, according to
'thofe rules of reafon and juftice, which the ftate and circumftances of their af-
'fairs may require, and mutually point out; provided neverthelefs that thofe
'conditions are not repugnant to the defigns and equitable intentions of their
'Sovereigns for the peace and reconciliation of the two Crowns.

10. 'The demand of the reftitution of the captures at fea before the decla-
'ration of war cannot be admitted; fuch a claim not being founded on any par-
'ticular convention, and by no means refulting from the law of nations, as
'there is no principle more conteftible than this, viz. that the abfolute right of
'all hoftile operations does not refult from a formal declaration of war, but
'from the hoftilities which the aggreffor has firft offered.

11. 'As the indifpenfable care which is due from his Majefty to his people,
'and the juft and invincible motives which concern the prefervation and fecuri-
'ty of his kingdoms, authorized by the moft formal ftipulations of folemn trea-
'ties (viz. thofe of Radftadt, and the Barriere) and even by the exprefs and irre-
'vocable conditions of the ceffion of the Low Countries, will not allow France
'to retain poffeffion of Oftend and Newport, the two places aforefaid fhall be
'eva-

' evacuated, without delay, by the French garrisons; it is for this reason de-
' clared that the restitutions spoken of in the preceding Articles of this Memo-
' rial, and particularly the convention which is to be framed and regulated with re-
' spect to the Indies, cannot take place till the aforesaid evacuation of Ostend
' and Newport shall be faithfully executed.

12. ' The cessation of arms between the two crowns shall be fixed and take
' place on the day of the ratification of the preliminaries, or of the definitive
' treaty, and all the Articles relative to the cessation of hostilities, shall be set-
' tled and take place, according to common usage in such cases, and as the cir-
' cumstances in different parts of the world shall require.

13. ' His Majesty having, from the first overtures made on the part of France,
' declared, that in case the separate peace between the two Crowns should be
' concluded, his Majesty would continue, as an Auxiliary, faithfully to assist the
' King of Prussia, with efficacy and good faith, in order to accomplish the sa-
' lutary purpose of a general pacification in Germany; it shall be free to Great
' Britain and France, to support, as Auxiliaries, their respective Allies, in their
' particular contests for the recovery of Silesia, pursuant to the respective en-
' gagements which those Crowns have entered into.

14. ' The prisoners taken on one side and the other, both by sea and land,
' shall be released in the usual manner, saving the terms which may exist by vir-
' tue of some cartel or some convention, which may have relation to this par-
' ticular.

' These articles are not digested into the form, nor in the detail of articles of
' peace; but it is hoped that, with regard to essential points, this Memorial has
' that precision and perspicuity which leaves nothing doubtful, and which evi-
' dently demonstrates the sincerity and perseverance of his Majesty's disposition,
' with respect to his intentions and resolutions for the accomplishment of so great
' a blessing as that of an entire peace between the two Crowns.

The first article of this sketch entirely deprived the French of the liberty of
fishing for cod; and the demolition of Dunkirk required in the 4th article, only restored this liberty in part, with certain limitations and under certain restrictions which were not explained.

From the second article, one might infer that England pretended, not only
to keep an exclusive possession of all Canada, but also to make herself mistress of
all the Neutral Countries between Canada and Louisiana, to be nearer at hand
in order to invade the last Colony when she should think proper.

The third Article confirmed the entire possession of the African Coast in favour
of the English, and deprived the French of all settlement in that part for the
Negroe trade.

The ninth entirely annihilated the French East India Company.

The seventh and thirteenth did not appear conclusive. In fact, by the first,
England proposed that France should evacuate Germany, and in the second she
agreed that the two Crowns should support their Allies in that part of Europe.

These answers, and all those which England has made in the course of the
' nego-

Negotiation, evidently manifest that the Court of London is averse to all reconciliation.

The Articles which declare the advantages which England would secure, are clear, decisive, and even dictatorial; those which concern the interests of France, are obscure, subject to various constructions, and leave a train of discussions, which, by leaving the source of the war still subsisting, would still have redounded to the prejudice of France, if she had agreed to admit the claims of England.

These reflections did not escape his Majesty's penetration. Nevertheless his Majesty, unwilling to take upon himself the rupture of a Negotiation, which, on his part, proposed the welfare of mankind, he ordered a Reply to be made to the Answer from England, Article by Article, in the following Memorial, in the form of an *Ultimatum.*

No. XXII.

Ultimatum of France in reply to that of England, of 5th of August, 1761.

Ultimatum of the Court of France, as a Reply to the Ultimatum of the Court of England, remitted to the D. de Choiseul by M. Stanley.

' THE King renews the Declaration which he made to his Britannic Majesty, to the Memorial of Propositions for Peace, which has been transmitted to M. Stanley, and to which the Court of England has given no Answer, either by word of mouth or in writing: his Majesty again declares, that if the Negotiation entered into at Paris and at London, for the re-establishment of Peace between the two Crowns, has not the desired success, all the Articles agreed to in that Negotiation by France, cannot be represented, on any occasion, as settled points, any more than the Memorial of the month of March last, relative to the *Uti possidetis.*

1. ' The King consents to cede Canada to England in the most extensive manner, as specified in the Memorial of Propositions; but his Majesty will not recede from the Conditions he has annexed to the same Memorial relative to the Catholic Religion, and to the power, facility, and liberty of emigration for the ancient subjects of the King. With regard to the Fishery in the Gulf of St. Laurence, the King means to maintain the immemorial right which his subjects have of fishing in the said Gulf, and of drying their fish on the Banks of Newfoundland, as it was agreed by the Treaty of Utrecht. As this Privilege would be granted in vain, if the French vessels had not some shelter appertaining to France in the Gulf, his Majesty proposed to the King of Great Britain the restitution of the Island of Cape Breton; he again proposes, either that island, or St. John, or such other Port, without Fortification, in the Gulf, or within reach of the Gulf, which may serve the French as a shelter, and secure to France the liberty of Fishing, from whence his Majesty has no intention to recede.

2. ' The King has in no part of his Memorial of propositions, affirmed that all which did not belong to Canada, appertained to Louisiana; it is even difficult
' cult

‘ cult to conceive such an assertion could be advanced. France, on the con-
‘ trary, demands that the intermediate nations between Canada and Louisiana, as
‘ also between Virginia and Louisiana, shall be considered as neutral nations, in-
‘ dependant of the Sovereignty of the two Crowns, and serve as a barrier between
‘ them. If the English Minister would have attended to the instructions of M.
‘ Bussy on this subject, he would have seen that France agreed with England as
‘ to this proposition.

3. ‘ No answer has been given by England to the plain argument, That if Se-
‘ negal cannot be enjoyed in security without Goree, England will make no great
‘ sacrifice, in keeping Goree, and restoring Senegal to France Upon this ar-
‘ ticle, Mr. Stanley has acquainted the D. de Choiseul that some expedients may be
‘ agreed on between the two Crowns: in consequence of which his Majesty, out
‘ of regard to the blessing of peace, has authorized M. Bussy to treat concern-
‘ ing these expedients with the British Ministry.

4. ‘ The Court of London, when they mean to secure, in pursuance of his Ma-
‘ jesty’s consent, the conquests they pretend to maintain, readily rely on the Me-
‘ morial of *Uti Possidetis*; but they take no notice of that Memorial when they
‘ advance claims at the expence of France.   It cannot be denied but that the state
‘ of the town of Dunkirk is not included in the *Uti Possidetis.*

‘ According to the Treaty of Utrecht, the Demolition of Dunkirk was not as-
‘ sented to, as a compensation for the liberty of drying codfish on the Banks of
‘ Newfoundland ; it is the cession of Newfoundland, on the part of France, which
‘ is the ground of that compensation : but the King, to testify to all Europe, his
‘ sincere desire of peace, and to remove all obstacles which the enemies to peace
‘ may throw in the way, authorizes his Minister at London to negotiate con-
‘ cerning the state of Dunkirk, so soon as a convenient port shall be agreed up-
‘ on in the Gulf of St. Lawrence, or within reach of the Gulf, which shall be
‘ ceded to France, to serve as a shelter for her fishing vessels.

5. ‘ France has refuted the title of England to the Antilles, which are pretend-
‘ ed to be neutral ; His Majesty nevertheless, from a principle of moderation,
‘ accepts of the partition of the said islands ; but such partition cannot take place
‘ but in the form specified in the first Memorial of the French propositions.

6. ‘ It seems as if England, by her propositions, offered the island of Belleisle as
‘ a compensation for the island of Minorca : as France does not allow the impor-
‘ tance of the conquest of Belleisle, the two Courts will retain their several opi-
‘ nions ; England shall maintain her conquest, and France shall keep Mi-
‘ norca.

7. ‘ France is willing to evacuate, in consideration of the restitution to be made
‘ by England of the Island of Guadaloupe and of Marigalante, the countries
‘ belonging to the Landgrave of Hesse, to the Duke of Brunswic, and to the
‘ Electorate of Hanover, which are or shall be occupied by his Majesty’s forces,
‘ and of which the conquest is connected with the British War, since the rupture
‘ of the capitulation of Closter Seven, and which may be separated from the War
‘ of the Empress-Queen with the King of Prussia.

F

‘ But

' But as to what concerns Wesel, Gueldres, and other countries in Westphalia
' belonging to the King of Pruffia, which are actually in poffeffion of the Em-
' prefs-Queen, and where juftice is adminiftered in the name of her Imperial
' Majefty, the King cannot ftipulate to furrender the Conquefts of his Allies ; and
' fuch an evacuation, neither in fact nor by right, can take place without the
' confent of the Emprefs Queen at the Congrefs at Augfburg; that Congrefs be-
' ing to affemble in order to terminate the differences which have arifen in the
' Empire, and particularly thofe which have occafioned the War between her
' Imperial Majefty and the King of Pruffia.

8. ' The King accepts on thefe conditions ; and in confideration of the ceffions
' made by France, in North America and Africa, as well as in regard to the fet-
' tlement of Dunkirk, the reftitution of the Ifland of Guadaloupe and of Mari-
' galante.

9. ' The French Eaft-India Company have fulfilled the conditions of the
' Treaty made between Meff. Godeheu and Saunders : that of England has not
' obferved the fame punctuality. However that may be, the King is willing to
' acquiefce in the 9th Article of the *Ultimatum* of England, in relation to Afia.

10. ' The King perfifts, with regard to the Captures made before the War, in
' the contents of the 12th Article of the firft Propofitions. M. Buffy is autho-
' rifed to deliver a Memorial exprefsly on this fubject ; and every one is perfua-
' ded in France, that this object neither can nor ought to break off the Negotia-
' tion between the two Crowns.

11. ' The Emprefs-Queen enjoys full fovereignty in the towns of Oftend and
' Neuport ; the King has only lent his forces to his Ally to fecure thofe places.
' England has no right to impofe laws upon the King and the Emprefs, contrary
' to the will of the King and of her Imperial Majefty, who do not in the leaft
' violate the Treaties of the Houfe of Auftria with the States General. As to
' what remains, his Majefty readily declares, that his intention never was to
' keep poffeffion of the faid places after the eftablifhment of peace.

12. ' The 12th Article of the *Ultimatum* of England does not feem liable to
' any difficulties, while the terms of the intended Sufpenfion fhall be obferved
' and maintained with fincerity.

13. ' In anfwer to the Declaration made by Mr. Stanley, that in cafe of a fe-
' parate Peace between France and England, his Britannic Majefty would con-
' ftantly continue, in the capacity of an Auxiliary, to aid his Ally the King of
' Pruffia with all his power, and with the utmoft integrity, in order to accom-
' plifh the happy iffue of the War, and the pacification of Germany, the D. de
' Choifeul, in the name of the King, his Mafter, has declared to Mr. Stanley,
' that his Majefty, with the fame view to the general pacification, will alfo fup-
' port his faithful Allies with all his forces, and to the utmoft of his power, and
' will take every precaution which his approved fincerity and integrity fhall fug-
' geft to him, in order to prevent the feparate Peace of France with England
' from being prejudicial to them.
' It is in confequence of thefe fentiments, that the King, with the confent of
' his Allies, is willing to ftipulate, that he will grant no fuccour of any kind to
' his

7

' his Allies for the continuance of their War againſt the King of Pruſſia; but his
' Majeſty neither can nor will enter into ſuch an engagement, unleſs his Britannic
' Majeſty will enter into the like agreement with reſpect to the King of Pruſſia.

' The Propoſition of leaving France at liberty to ſend forces into Sileſia, is
' unfavourable, from particular circumſtances, to the intereſts of the Empreſs,
' and conſequently inadmiſſible.

' The King, therefore, perſiſts in the Propoſitions contained in the 10th Ar-
' ticle of his firſt Memorial. All that can be negotiated with reſpect to theſe
' points, muſt be the liberty of affording ſuccours in money to the reſpective Al-
' lies, ſo ſoon as it ſhall be poſitively aſcertained that no power ſhall be at liberty
' to furniſh them any ſupplies of men, or warlike ſtores, under any denomina-
' tion whatever.

14. ' The King accepts the 14th Article of the *Ultimatum* of England.

' It is hoped that the Court of Great Britain, will allow the preciſion of the
' Anſwers to their *Ultimatum*, as well as the readineſs with which the King endea-
' vours, even to his prejudice, to uſe all means to bring about a reconciliation
' with the King of Great Britain.'

M. Buſſy, on preſenting his *Ultimatum*, accompanied it with the following
Letter, in Anſwer to that of Mr. Pitt, of the 24th of July.

No. XXIII.
Mr. Buſſy's letter to Mr. Pitt, 5th Auguſt, 1761.

' SIR,

' I Have acquainted my Court with the Letter of the 24th of laſt month, with
' which your Excellency honoured me, on returning the Memorial I laid be-
' fore you, in relation to the intereſts of the Court of Spain with reſpect to
' England, and the Note which I thought it my duty to communicate, with re-
' gard to the intention of the King my Maſter, concerning the neceſſary ſteps
' to put a ſtop to hoſtilities in Germany.

' The King, Sir, orders me to acquaint your Excellency, that as to what
' relates to the intereſt of the Catholic King, his Majeſty's precaution expreſſed
' in the Memorial which I remitted to you, is in conſequence of that ſincerity
' which he profeſſes conſtantly to adopt in the courſe of all his Negotiations.
' The Memorial which your Excellency has returned me, neither contains any
' menaces, nor any offer of mediation. No other ſentiment can be inferred from
' it, than that of the ſincere deſire which his Majeſty entertains, that the pro-
' jected peace between France and England, may be firm and durable. More-
' over, the King refers himſelf to his Catholic Majeſty concerning the manner in
' which this Memorial was received and remitted ; but his Majeſty has charged
' me to declare to your Excellency, that ſo long as Spain ſhall approve of it,
' his Majeſty will interfere with the intereſts of that Crown, without deſiſting on
' account of a repulſe from the Power who oppoſes his good offices.   ' With

' With respect to the matter of the Note, likewise returned by your Excellen-
' cy, and which relates to the two necessary conditions of the proposed expe-
' dient for evacuating the countries subdued by his Majesty's arms, his Ma-
' jesty explains himself fully on that Article in the *Ultimatum*, in Answer to that
' of the Court of London. His Majesty has ordered me to declare further to
' you in writing, that he will rather sacrifice the Power which God has given
' him, than conclude any thing with his enemies, which may be contrary to the
' engagements he has contracted, and that good faith in which he glories. If
' England will undertake to yield no succour to the King of Prussia, the King
' will engage, on the other hand, to afford none to his Allies in Germany.
' But his Majesty will not adopt the liberty of succouri g his Allies with a sup-
' ply of men, because he is sensible of the disadvantage which the present situa-
' tion of the armies might occasion to the Empress Queen. His Majesty may sti-
' pulate not to act for the benefit of his Allies, but he neither can or will con-
' sent to any condition which may be detrimental to them.

' It remains for me to observe to your Excellency, how greatly my court was
' astonished, as well at the stile of the Letter you wrote to me, as at the *Ulti-*
' *matum* of England. This stile, which is so little conformable to the proposi-
' tions of France, betrays the aversion of the Court of London to peace. The
' King, who is very far from insisting on forms, when the happiness of Eu-
' rope is at stake, has used every endeavour, in the Answer to the *Ultimatum*,
' which, without injury to the honour of his Crown, were judged most effectual
' to recall the British Court to sentiments of pacification : your Excellency will
' judge, from the *Ultimatum* of France, that I am ordered to acquaint you with
' what facility the King, forgetting the imperative stile, so unfit for Negotia-
' tion, which England makes use of in her Answers, enters into the views of
' the British Court, and endeavours, by the sacrifices he makes, to engage them
' to adopt the stipulations of a reasonable peace.

' If your Excellency is desirous of having a conference with me on the sub-
' ject of the *Ultimatum*, I will attend your commands, and I shall be very ear-
' nest to testify the disposition of my Court, to make a happy issue of the Nego-
' tiation on foot, as also the peculiar regard with which, &c.

' Signed De Buffy.'

At length, as the British Ministry had seemed to resent the Memorial relative
to Spain, his Catholic Majesty authorized his Ambassador at London, the Count
of Fuentes, to remit the following Note to Mr. Pitt, which is the interpretation
of the Memorial.

No. XXIV.

Note of the Spanish Ambassador to Mr. Pitt.

' THE Most Christian King, who wishes to make the peace, concerning which
' he proposed to treat with England, at once effectual and durable, entrust-
' ed his intentions with the King my Master, expressing the pleasure with which

' he

' he embraced that opportunity of acknowledging his fenfe of the reiterated of-
' fers which his Catholic Majefty had made both to Him and England, in order
' to facilitate a juft and lafting reconciliation.

' It is from thefe principles of fincerity that the Moft Chriftian King propofed
' to the King my Mafter the guaranty of the Treaty of Peace, as a meafure
' which might be equally convenient to France and England, and at the fame
' time affured him of his fincere intentions with refpect to the facrifices he pro-
' pofed to make, in order to reftore tranquillity to Europe, by an honourable
' and lafting peace.

' Such a proceeding of his Moft Chriftian Majefty could not but be highly ac-
' ceptable to the King my Mafter, who found it agreeable to his own fentiments,
' and to his defire of fulfilling on his part, with the moft diftinguifhed conformity,
' all the connections which unite them both by ties of blood and their mutual
' intereft ; and moreover, he perceived in the difpofition of the King of France,
' that magnanimity and humanity which are natural to him, by his endeavours,
' on his fide, to render the Peace as permanent as the viciffitudes of human affairs
' will admit of.

' It is with the fame candor and fincerity that the King my Mafter expreffed
' in confidence to the Moft Chriftian King, that he wifhed his Britannic Majefty
' had not made a difficulty of fettling the guaranty, on account of the grievances
' of Spain with England, as he has all the reafon to conclude that his Britannic
' Majefty has the fame good intentions to terminate them amicably, according to
' reafon and juftice.

' The confidence which the King my Mafter repofed in France, gave that
' Court room to teftify to his Britannic Majefty the fincerity of their intentions
' for the re-eftablifhment of peace, fince, by propofing the guaranty of Spain, they
' expreffed their fincere defire of feeing the interefts of Spain fettled at the fame
' time, which might one day re-kindle the flames of a new war, which at prefent
' they wifh to extinguifh.

' If the intentions of the Moft Chriftian King and the King my Mafter did
' not feem fraught with fincerity, the King my Mafter flatters himfelf, that his
' Britannic Majefty will do him the juftice to confider his in that light, fince,
' if they were founded on any other principle, his Catholic Majefty giving full
' fcope to his greatnefs, would have fpoken from himfelf, and as became his
' dignity.

' I muft not omit to inform you, that the King my Mafter will learn with fur-
' prize, that the Memorial of France could raife a fentiment in the breaft of his
' Britannic Majefty, entirely oppofite to the intentions of the two Sovereigns.

' But his Catholic Majefty will always be pleafed, whenever he fees that they
' make that progrefs which he has ever defired, in the Negociation of Peace,
' whether it be feparate between France and England, or general ; as his fincere
' wifhes are to make it perpetual, by obviating every fource which might here-
' after unhappily renew the war.

' For this reafon, the King my Mafter flatters himfelf that his Britannic
' Majefty, animated with the fame fentiments of humanity towards the public
' tran-

' tranquillity, will exprefs the same intentions of terminating the difputes of
' England with a power which has afforded fuch reiterated proofs of her friend-
' fhip, at the fame time that it is propofed to reftore peace to all Europe in ge-
' neral.

The King ordered M. Buffy, by the inftructions which were fent to him with
the *Ultimatum*, to agree to the ceffion of Canada, in the full extent which England defired it, fo that the fifhery on the coaft and in the Gulf of St. Lawrence was maintained to France, and that England would appoint a port in
that part, which might be fubject to the fovereignty of his Majefty, and ferve
the French fifhermen for a fhelter.

M. Buffy had in charge to agree upon the limits of Canada and Louifiana, according to the Englifh map, though very unfavourable to the rights and poffeffions
of France. With regard to Africa, the King's Minifter was authorized to confent
to the ceffion required by England, fo that the exportation of negroes might be
confirmed to France by fome expedients equally eafy and fure ; and his Majefty
made the facrifice of Dunkirk, in compenfation of the fecurity of fifhing in the
Gulf of St. Lawrence, in favour of his fubjects.

As to what concerns Afia, the King authorized M. Buffy to agree that the
French and Englifh India companies, fhould adjuft their refpective interefts
among themfelves, upon condition that they fufpend hoftilities during the Negotiation, and that the advantages on either fide fhould be confidered as a compenfation with regard to the refpective interefts of the two Crowns.

The King infifted, in the Inftructions he fent to his Minifter at London,
upon the Article refpecting the Reftitution of the French veffels taken before the
war by the Englifh marine. His Majefty's love for his fubjects would not
allow him to omit any thing to alleviate the diftreffes which feveral towns in his
kingdom fuftained by means of thofe illegal captures. M. Buffy had even orders
to prefent the following Memorial on that fubject.

No. XXV.

Memorial concerning the Veffels taken before the War.

Concerning the Reclaim of the Prizes made before the Declaration of the War.

' THE Reclaim of the Captures made by the Englifh before the Declaration
' of War, is founded on the Treaties of Utrecht and Aix la Chapelle.

' It is not neceffary to conteft the principle that the right of exercifing Ho-
' ftilities does not always refult from the formality of a Declaration of war; but
' as it is impracticable for two Princes who make war on each other, to agree
' between them which is the aggreffor with regard to the other, equity and hu-
' manity have dictated thefe precautions, that where an unforefeen rupture hap-
' pens fuddenly, and without any previous declaration, foreign veffels, which,
' navigating under the fecurity of peace and of treaties, happen at the time of
' the rupture to be in either of the refpective ports, fhall have time and full
' liberty to withdraw themfelves.

' This

' This wise provision, so agreeable to the rules of good faith, constitutes a
' part of the Law of Nations, and the Article of the Treaty which sanctifies
' these precautions ought to be faithfully executed, notwithstanding the breach
' of the other Articles of the Treaty, which is the natural consequence of the
' war.

' The Courts of France and Great Britain used this salutary precaution in the
' Treaties of Utrecht and Aix la Chapelle ; in the first, by the nineteenth Ar-
' ticle of the Treaty of Peace, and in the second of the Treaty of Commerce :
' in the second, by the third Article which renews and confirms the first.

' If these Treaties allow a protection to the respective subjects who may have
' ships in the ports of either of the Powers, because, having no opportunity of
' knowing that a rupture has fallen out, they sailed under the Security of Peace
' and under the Faith of Treaties ; by a parity of reason, all the other subjects
' who are not inhabitants of the respective ports, who have ships at sea,
' should enjoy the same security for their vessels, in whatever part of the sea
' they should be sailing, otherwise it would follow, that the Sovereigns provide
' for the preservation of one part of their subjects from the miseries of a sudden
' rupture, to which they expose the rest, which is absolutely repugnant to the
' humanity of Sovereigns, and contrary to right reason.

' It is upon this principle that the King of France restored to England the
' English Vessels which were found in the ports of France, at the time of the
' rupture, or taken at sea before the Declaration of War.

' If his Majesty had not caused those vessels to be restored, his Britannic Ma-
' jesty might have alledged that he retained the French vessels by way of Re-
' prisals ; but the punctuality of France in conforming to the Treaties of Utrecht
' and Aix la Chapelle, and to the principles resulting from thence, give England
' no pretence for refusing to fulfil engagements which are reciprocal.

' The Court of France therefore does not doubt but that the Court of Eng-
' land will agree to order the Restitution of the ships taken by the English from
' the French, before the Declaration of the War."

The King likewise ordered his Minister to represent, with its full force, the
utility which would redound to the two Crowns by the total desertion of the war
in Germany. His Majesty moreover required M. Bussy, after having used his
utmost endeavours to persuade the British Ministry to acquiesce in propositions
so advantageous to England, to wait for fresh instructions, if the Court of London should refuse the conditions offered in the *Ultimatum* of France, the King
being resolved to carry his compliance as far as possible, in order to inspire the
King of England with pacific dispositions.

The *Ultimatum* of France, of the 5th August, arrived at London the 8th of
the same month : M. Bussy wrote to Mr. Pitt : that Minister returned him the
following Answer on the 15th.

No. XXVI.

Mr. Pitt's Letter to M. Bussy. 15th *August,* 1761.

SIR,

'I Made the King my Master acquainted with the Memorial, which, by the or-
'der of his Most Christian Majesty, you accompanied the *Ultimatum* of the
'Court of France: his Majesty perceives from these two pieces, with that regret
'with which the love of peace inspires him, that the happy moment to put an
'end to so many miseries is not yet come.

'As to what relates to the stile of the *Ultimatum* of England in answer to the
'Memorial of propositions from France, as likewise of the letter which I ad-
'dressed to you by his Majesty's order, upon returning the two papers relative
'to Spain and the King of Prussia, as totally inadmissible, the King orders me to ac-
'quaint, you, Sir, that his Majesty adheres both to the form and substance of
'those two pieces, in which his dignity concurred with his justice and good
'faith, leaving all the world to judge which of the two Courts have shewn an aver-
'sion to peace during the course of the Negotiation; whether it be that Court, which
'from a principle of candour, not by way of assuming an imperative tone, has
'always endeavoured to give open answers, in order to shorten delays, by ob-
'viating misunderstandings, and to avoid the reproach of having acted delu-
'sively even with an enemy; who, in the conditions of peace, so far from mak-
'ing an ill use of her prosperity, has not even insisted on all those rights which the
'*Uti possidetis,* and the Memorial of France of the 26th March, gave her;
'who, moreover, proposes, that after the conclusion of peace between the two
'Crowns they shall respectively be at liberty, with regard to the contest concern-
'ing Silesia, to fulfil the engagements they have contracted with their Allies;
'it belongs therefore, Sir, to Europe to judge whether this is the Court which
'has shewn an aversion to peace, or whether it is not that, which after so many
'variations and delays on her part, arbitrarily continues to insist on objects in
'America which we have a right to by the *Uti possidetis,* and which would make
'a direct attempt on the essential rights of our conquests of Canada and its
'appurtenances, in the Gulf of St. Laurence; which, in Germany, not only
'refuses to give up her conquests, gained over his Majesty's Allies, as a just
'compensation for the important restitutions with which his Majesty is willing
'to accommodate France, but even pretends to impose an obligation on his Ma-
'jesty not to fulfil the engagements of his Crown towards the King of Prussia;
'which moreover, not satisfied with throwing so many insuperable obstacles in
'the way to peace, has not scrupled to interpose new perplexities in opposition
'to this precious blessing for which the nations sigh, by intermixing, too late,
'matters so foreign to the present Negotiation between the two Crowns, as are
'the discussions between Great Britain and Spain.

'Such, Sir, being the conduct of the two Courts, the King perceives with
'regret that the peace so much desired is far distant, and that at this very mo-
'ment

' ment the Court of France is willing to intruft it to the uncertain fate of far-
' ther events.

' If this is the intention of France, his Majefty relies on the fame Providence,
' which has hitherto bleffed his arms, and the fincerity of his intentions to-
' wards peace; and hopes, that the courfe of events, accomplifhing what his
' Majefty's moderation has in vain attempted, will recal the Court of France to
' a more favourable difpofition.

' Neverthelefs, Sir, although I am not at liberty to confer with you concern-
' ing the *Ultimatum* of your Court feparately, yet if you defire, Sir, that we
' fhould have a conference on the two *Ultimatums* of our Courts together, I will
' be at your command when you think proper, that I may have the honour to
' learn what you have to communicate to me with refpect to the intentions of
' your Court.

' I have the Honour to be, *&c.*

Signed   W. Pitt.

Europe will be able to judge by the pieces contained in this Memorial, and
which cannot be difavowed by the Britifh Miniftry, any more than their dates,
whether France has ufed any delay in the Negotiation, and whether fhe has va-
ried from her propofitions, and from the conftant defire fhe has always expreffed
for the conclufion of peace.

No. XXVII.

Mr. Buffy's Anfwer to Mr. Pitt, 16th Auguft, 1761.

S I R,

' I Received the letter which your Excellency did me the honour to write to me
' on the 16th of this month. I will not undertake to difcufs the principal
' object of it without fubmitting it to my Court, whether it is proper to make
' a reply, and what that reply fhould be. I will confine myfelf, Sir, to affure
' you that I accept, with pleafure, the offer your Excellency makes me of a
' Conference on the fubject of the two *Ultimatums* of our Courts; as you are
' out of town, and as I would not trefpafs on the moments you devote to the
' eftablifhment of your health, I refer myfelf to you entirely to appoint the day
' and hour when I may come to confer with you.

' Nothing can be more true than the affurance I make to you of the refpect-
' ful attachment with which you have infpired me, and with which I have the
' Honour to be, &c.

Signed,   De Buffy.

The many deliberations of the Britifh Court, and the delay, from the 8th to
the 30th of the fame month, of the Anfwer to the *Ultimatum* of France, renewed
the hopes of reconciliation between the two Crowns. At length the Anfwer came,
and Mr. Stanley remitted it on the 1ft of September to the Duke de Choifeul.

G   No.

No. XXVIII.

The Anſwer of England to the Ultimatum of France, received the 1ſt September, 1761

The Anſwer of the Britiſh Court to the *Ultimatum* of the Court of France, re-mitted the 17th of Auguſt, by M. Buſſy Miniſter Plenipotentiary of the Moſt Chriſtian King, to the Secretary of State of his Britannic Majeſty of the South-ern department.

'THE Moſt Chriſtian King having repeatedly declared, in the *Ultimatum* of
' the Court of France, remitted to Mr. Pitt by M. Buſſy, as well as in the
' Memorial of the propoſitions of peace, which was remitted by the Duke de
' Choiſeul to Mr. Stanley, that, if the Negotiation entered upon between the two
' Crowns has not the deſired effect, all the Articles conceded in that Negotia-
' tion by France, cannot be conſidered in any caſe as points agreed upon, any
' more than the Memorial of the month of March laſt, in relation to the *Uti*
' *poſſidetis*; the King declares, in return, that if the conceſſions his Majeſty has
' made to bring about peace, ſhould not be accepted by his moſt Chriſtian Ma-
' jeſty, the important reſtitutions offered to France, as well as the other circum-
' ſtances herein after expreſſed, cannot for the future be conſidered as given up.

Article I.

' The King will not deſert his claim to the entire and total Ceſſion of all Cana-
' da and its dependencies, without any new limits or exceptions whatever; and
' likewiſe inſiſts on the compleat ceſſion of the Iſland of Cape Breton, and of the
' other Iſlands in the gulf and river of St. Laurence.

' Canada, according to the lines of its limits, traced by the Marquis de Vau-
' dreuil himſelf, when that Governor ſurrendered the ſaid province by capitula-
' tion to the Britiſh General Sir J. Amherſt, comprehends on one ſide the lakes
' Huron, Michigan and Superieur; and the ſaid line drawn to the Red Lake,
' takes in, by a ſerpentine progreſs, the river Ouabachi, as far as its junction
' with the Ohio, and from thence extends itſelf along the latter river as far in-
' cluſively as its influx into the Miſſiſſippi.

' It is in conformity to this ſtate of the limits made by the French Governor,
' that the King claims the Ceſſion of Canada, a province which the Court of
' France moreover has offered anew by their *Ultimatum*, to cede to his Britan-
' nic Majeſty, *in the moſt extenſive manner, as expreſſed in the Memorial of Propo-*
' *ſitions of Peace, of 13th July.*

' As to what concerns the public profeſſion and exerciſe of the Roman Ca-
' tholic religion in Canada, the new ſubjects of his Britannic Majeſty ſhall be
' maintained in that privilege without interruption or moleſtation; and the French
' inhabitants, or others, who may have been ſubjects of the Moſt Chriſtian King
' in Canada, ſhall have full liberty and power to ſell their effects, provided they
' diſpoſe of them to the ſubjects of his Britannic Majeſty, and to tranſport their
' property, as well as their perſons, without being reſtrained from their emi-
' gration under any pretence whatever; (unleſs in caſe of debt, or for the breach
' of criminal laws;) it being always underſtood, that the time granted for the

3   ' ſaid

' said emigration shall be limited to the space of one year, to be computed
' from the day of the Ratification of the Definitive Treaty.

II.

' As to what respects the line to be drawn from Rio-Perdido, as contained
' in the Note remitted by M. Bussy of the 18th of this month, with regard to
' the Limits of Louisiana, his Majesty is obliged to reject so unexpected a pro-
' position, as by no means admissible in two respects.

1. ' Because the said line, under colour of fixing the limits of Louisiana, an-
' nexes vast countries to that province, which with the commanding posts and
' forts, the Marquis de Vandreuil has, by the most solemn capitulation, incon-
' testibly yielded into the possession of his Britannic Majesty, under the descrip-
' tion of Canada, and that consequently, however contentious the pretensions of
' the two Crowns may have been before the war, and particularly with respect
' to the course of the Ohio, and the territories in that part since the surrender
' of Canada, and the line of its limits has been traced as aforesaid by the Mar-
' quis de Vandreuil, all those opposite titles are united, and become valid without
' contradiction, to confirm to Great Britain, with all the rest of Canada, the pos-
' session of those countries on that part of the Ohio which have been heretofore
' contested.

2. " The line proposed to fix the Bounds of Louisiana cannot be admitted, be-
' cause it would comprize in another part, on the side of the Carolinas, very
' extensive countries and numerous nations, who have always been reputed to
' be under the protection of the King, a right which his Majesty has no inten-
' tion of renouncing ; and then the King, for the advantage of peace, might con-
' sent to leave the intermediate countries under the protection of Great Britain,
' and particularly the Cherokees, the Creeks, the Chicasaws, the Chactaws, and
' another nation, situate between the British settlements and the Missisippi.

III.

' The King refers to the third Article of the *Ultimatum* of England concerning
' the Cession of Senegal and its dependencies, as well as the island of Goree, in
' the most ample manner, as expressed in the said article ; and his Majesty re-
' news the declaration which has been made by Mr. Stanley, that if the Court of
' France would suggest any reasonable expedient to provide themselves with
' Negroes, which may not be too detrimental to the interests of the British sub-
' jects in Africa, he will willingly enter upon a discussion of this subject.

IV.

' The important privilege granted by the 13th article of the treaty of Utrecht,
' under certain limitations and restrictions, to the subjects of France for fishing
' and drying their cod fish on a certain part of the banks of Newfoundland, has
' not been refused by Great Britain, but connected with a reciprocal satisfaction on
' the part of France, with regard to the indispensable object of Dunkirk, which
' the King has required, and still requires : it is therefore on condition that the

' town

' Town and Port of Dunkirk shall be put in the condition it ought to have been
' in by the last treaty of Aix la Chapelle, that his Majesty consents to renew to
' France the privilege of fishing and of drying their fish by virtue of the trea-
' ty of Utrecht, upon the aforesaid district of Newfoundland.

' As to the demand which his Most Christian Majesty has farther made that
' his subjects may fish in the Gulf of St. Laurence, as also to have a port there
' *without fortifications*, and subject to the inspection of England, as proposed on
' the part of the D. de Choiseul in his conferences with Mr. Stanley on that
' head, which port should merely serve as a shelter to the fishing boats of the
' French nation which shall land there ; the King, to manifest to his Most Chris-
' tian Majesty and to the whole world, the sincerity of his intentions with regard
' to peace, will consent,

1. ' To grant the French subjects the privilege of fishing in the Gulf of St.
' Laurence, upon this express condition, that is to say ; That the said French
' subjects shall abstain from that particular fishery on all the coasts appertaining
' to Great Britain, whether on the Continent or on the Islands situated in the said
' Gulf of St. Laurence, which fishery the proprietors only of the said coasts
' have constantly enjoyed and always exercised; saving always the privilege grant-
' ed by the 13th article of the treaty of Utrecht, to the subjects of France to fish
' and dry their cod fish on a part specified on the Banks of Newfoundland,
' which privilege is proposed to be renewed to France as aforesaid.

2. ' The King will consent to cede to his Majesty the isle of St. Pierre with
' it's port, which isle, with respect to that part of Newfoundland situate be-
' tween the bay of Placentia and the bay of La Fortune, stands east south east,
' and its port opens towards the north east, the interior part of which port is
' called *Bourgway*; the isle of St. Pierre, which the King is willing to cede, is
' divided by a little streight from another island known by the name of *Ma-*
' *quelon*, or of *Michelon*, which lies to the north of the said isle of St. Pierre.

' To the cession of the said isle, as above mentioned, his Majesty annexes
' four indispensible conditions.

1. ' That France, on no pretence, nor under any denomination whatever,
' shall erect any fortifications, either in the said isle, or in its port, and that she
' shall not keep any troops there, nor maintain any military establishment what-
' ever.

2. ' That the said isle and the said port shall only serve as a shelter for the
' fishing vessels of the French nation, and that France shall not suffer the vessels
' of any other nation whatever to partake of the convenience of this shelter for
' the fishing boats.

3. ' That the possession of the isle of St. Pierre as aforesaid, shall not be con-
' strued in any case to confer, transmit, or participate in any manner whatever
' the least right or power of fishing or of drying cod fish in any part of the
' coast of Newfoundland, beyond the district expressly stipulated and fixed for
' that purpose by the 13th article of the treaty of Utrecht, that is to say, *a Loco*
' *Cap Bonavista nuncupato, usque ad extremitatem ejusdem Insulæ septentrionalem,*
' *indeque ad Latus occidentale recurrendo usque ad Lacum* Pointriche *appellatum.*

4. ' That

4. ' That in virtue of the ceſſion of the ſaid iſland as aforeſaid, an Engliſh
' commiſſary ſhall be allowed to reſide there, and the commander of the Bri-
' tiſh ſquadron at Newfoundland ſhall be at liberty from time to time to inſpect
' the ſaid iſle and the ſaid port, to ſee that the ſtipulations above expreſſed are
' punctually obſerved.

V.

' The propoſition of an alternative ſuggeſted by the Court of France, in rela-
' tion to the iſles of Tobago, St. Lucia, Dominica, and St. Vincent, common-
' ly called Neutral iſlands, is by no means admiſſible. The King however,
' from a principle of moderation, continues his inclination to agree to an equal
' partition of the ſaid four iſlands, to be aſcertained in the future treaty between
' the two Crowns.

VI.

' The King conſents to reſtore to his Moſt Chriſtian Majeſty,

1. ' The important conqueſt of Belle-Iſle, with the artillery, &c. which was
' therein at the time of taking the ſaid Iſland.

2. ' His Majeſty likewiſe agrees to reſtore to the Moſt Chriſtian King the fer-
' tile and wealthy Iſland of Guadaloupe, with that of Marigalante, with the
' artillery, &c. which was therein at the time of taking the ſaid Iſlands.

VII.

' The Iſland of Minorca ſhall be reſtored to his Britannic Majeſty, as likewiſe
' Fort St. Philip, in the condition it ſtood, and with the artillery therein, &c. at
' the time of taking the ſaid Iſland and Fort.

VIII.

' As to what regards the reſtitution and evacuation of the Conqueſts made by
' France over the King's Allies in Germany, and particularly of Weſel and the
' other territories of the King of Pruſſia, his Majeſty perſiſts in his demand re-
' lative to that ſubject in the 7th Article of the *Ultimatum* of England ; it being
' always underſtood, that all the places belonging to his Majeſty's Allies in Ger-
' many ſhall be reſtored, with the artillery, &c. found in them at the time of
' taking the ſaid places.

IX.

' With regard to the ſuccour to be afforded to the King of Pruſſia on the part
' of the Britiſh Crown, as an Auxiliary, after the concluſion of the ſeparate
' Peace between Great Britain and France, his Majeſty remains in the ſame in-
' flexible reſolution, which he declared at the firſt overture of the preſent Nego-
' tiation, that he will never deſiſt from giving conſtant ſuccour to the King of
' Pruſſia, as an Auxiliary, *with Efficacy and good Faith*, in order to attain the ſa-
' lutary end of a general Pacification in Germany. With this view, his Majeſty,
' far from propoſing to leave France at liberty to ſend armies into Sileſia, *with-*
' *out being limited to the number ſtipulated in her actual engagements with the Court*
' *of Vienna*, (a circumſtance not to be found in any part of the *Ultimatum* of Eng-
' land) has uniformly declared, as the 13th Article of the ſaid *Ultimatum* pro-
' feſſes, that Great Britain and France ſhall be at liberty to ſupport their reſpec-

tive

' tive Allies as Auxiliaries, in their particular conteſt for the recovery of Sileſia,
' according to the engagements entered into by each Crown.

' The King declares at the ſame time, that his Majeſty has neither the inten-
' tion nor the authority to take upon him to inhibit and forbid any foreign troops
' from entering into the ſervice and pay of the King of Pruſſia, however his
' Majeſty might be inclined to conſent not to furniſh, but by means of ſubſidy,
' thoſe ſupplies which Great Britain ſhall judge convenient to grant his Pruſſian
' Majeſty, in purſuance of her engagements.

X.

' With regard to the Captures made after the commencement of hoſtilities,
' and before the Declaration of War, the King continues of opinion, that ſuch a
' demand on the part of France is neither juſt nor maintainable, according to the
' moſt inconteſtible principles of the rights of War and of Nations.

XI.

' Concerning the evacuations of Oſtend and Nieuport, the King cannot but
' refer to the moſt expreſs and irrevocable ſtipulation of the moſt ſolemn Trea-
' ties, and expreſſed in the 11th Article of the *Ultimatum* of Great Britain, as alſo
' to his Declaration relative to that ſubject: and his Majeſty relies on the ſince-
' rity of the Declaration on the part of France; that is to ſay, that *the intention*
' *of his Moſt Chriſtian Majeſty never was to keep poſſeſſion of the aforeſaid places af-*
' *ter the return of Peace.*

XII.

' In regard to the ceſſation of hoſtilities, the King perſiſts, in every reſpect, in
' the ſame intentions, declared in the 12th Article of the Britiſh *Ultimatum.*

XIII.

' As to what concerns the French Eaſt-India Company, he can only refer to
' the 9th Article of the *Ultimatum* of England, with regard to which no diſagree-
' ment ſeems to ſubſiſt.

XIV.

' As to the priſoners of war, the two Courts ſeem to agree perfectly on that
' head.

' The Court of France cannot but perceive from this Anſwer, the ſincerity of
' his Majeſty's intentions, as well as the moderation which directs his Majeſty to-
' wards the means of reconciliation with the Moſt Chriſtian King.

Signed N. Stanley.

The D. de Choiſeul had ſeveral conferences with the Engliſh Miniſter on the
ſubject of this Anſwer; but M. Stanley, in thoſe conferences, as well as thro'
the whole courſe of the Negotiation, did not appear to be authorized by his Court
to come to any agreement with reſpect to the difficulties which occurred, nor
even to elucidate thoſe obſcurities which occurred in the Engliſh Anſwers, and
particularly in the 9th Article of the laſt Anſwer from the Court of London. As
this

this Minifter was confined to the letter of the Anfwer given by his Court, this circumftance abfolutely put a ftop to all eclairciffement on thefe points, and took away every expedient for removing the obftacles of the Negotiation. It was judged proper in France, in order to obviate thefe difficulties, to fend a new Memorial to England, as a final anfwer to the Court of London. This Memorial was fent to M. Buffy the 9th of September.

No. XXIX.

The laft Memorial of France to England, 9th September, 1761.

The Memorial of France to the Anfwer of England, tranfmitted to the D. de Choifeul the firft of September, by M. Stanley the Minifter of his Britannic Majefty.

‘ THE King accepts the Declaration of the King of England contained in
‘ the preamble of the Anfwer, and renews that which he before made to
‘ his Majefty on this head, in fuch manner that it is concluded between the two
‘ Courts finally and without ambiguity, that if peace is not the refult of the pre-
‘ fent Negotiation, all that has been faid, written and negotiated between the two
‘ Crowns, fince the Memorial of the 26th of March inclufive, to the moment
‘ of the rupture, fhall be void and of no effect, and fhall not be brought as an
‘ argument in favour of either of the parties, in any future negotiation of Peace.

Article I.

‘ The King has declared in his firft Memorial, and in his *Ultimatum*, That
‘ he will cede and guaranty to England, the poffeffion of Canada, in the moft
‘ ample manner; his Majefty perfifts in that offer, and without difcuffing the
‘ Line of its Limits marked in a map prefented by Mr. Stanley; as that line, on
‘ which England refts its demand, is without doubt the moft extenfive bound
‘ which can be given to the ceffion, the King is willing to grant it.

‘ His Majefty had annexed four conditions to his guarranty: it feems that
‘ England agrees to them; the King only conceives that the term of one year
‘ for the fale of the French effects and for the Emigration is too fhort, and his
‘ Majefty defires that it may be agreed to extend the term of one year to eighteen
‘ months at leaft.

‘ As the Court of England has added, to the firft article of their Anfwer to
‘ the entire and total Ceffion of Canada, as agreed between the two Courts, the
‘ word *Dependencies*, it is neceffary to give a fpecific explanation of this word,
‘ that the ceffion might not in the end occafion difficulties between the two Courts
‘ with regard to the meaning of the word Dependencies.

II.

‘ The firft paragraph, with refpect to the limits of Louifiana, contained in the
‘ fecond article of the Anfwer from England, is agreed to by France. The fe-
‘ cond

'cond paragraph is neither just nor explicit, and it is finally proposed to express
' it in the following terms.

' ' *The intermediate Savage Nations between the Lakes and the Mississippi, and with-*
' *in the Line traced out, shall be neuter and independent under the protection of the*
' *King, and those without the Line on the side of the English shall be likewise neuter*
' *and independant under the protection of the King of England. The English traders*
' *also shall be prohibited from going among the Savage Nations beyond the Line on*
' *either side ; but the said nations shall not be restrained in their freedom of commerce*
' *with the French and English, as they have exercised it heretofore.*

III.

' Although France is sensible how opposite it is to principles of conciliation,
' that the party which cedes should propose to the party who has conquered and
' would maintain the cession of possessions which are not perfectly known ; though
' there is no doubt but that the manner which England requires is liable to in-
' numerable difficulties, nevertheless the King, to testify his acquiescence in every
' expedient which may conciliate the two Crowns, is willing to declare to Eng-
' land, that he will guaranty the possession of Senegal and Goree to that Crown,
' provided England, on her part, will guaranty the possession of the settlements
' of Anamaboo and Akra, on the coast of Africa.

IV.

' The fourth article of the Answer includes variety of objects, each of which
' requires a particular explanation.
' England always endeavours to connect the liberty of fishing and of drying
' the fish on part of the coast of Newfoundland, granted by the fifteenth article
' of the Treaty of Utrecht, with the ninth article of the same Treaty, which sti-
' pulates the Demolition of Dunkirk : it is given in answer to England for the
' fourth and last time, that those two stipulations of the Treaty of Utrecht have
' nothing in common between them, unless that they are both comprized in
' the said Treaty ; and that the concession expressed in favour of the French in
' the thirteeth article of that Treaty, is a compensation for the cession of New-
' foundland and Annapolis Royal, made on the part of France to England by
' the twelfth and thirteenth articles of the same Treaty.
' But to the end that the two Courts may clearly understand each other on this
' head, and for the furtherance of Peace, the King agrees to demolish the works
' which have been made for the defence of the port of Dunkirk since the Begin-
' ning of this war, to fill up the bason which contains the ships of war, and to
' destroy the buildings belonging to the rope yard : but at the same time his
' Majesty will leave the trading port, which will not receive a frigate, subsisting
' for the good of England as well as for the benefit of France. She will also un-
' dertake not to suffer any maritime military establishment in that port ; but the
' cunette shall be left standing round the place for the salubrity of the air, and
' the health of the inhabitants.

' As

' As to the fishery and the drying of fish on the Banks of Newfoundland, the
' King requires that the thirteenth article of the Treaty of Utrecht be confirmed
' by the present Treaty.

' Concerning the condition proposed by England, with respect to the liberty
' of fishing in the Gulf of St. Lawrence, France agrees, that beyond the port of
' Newfoundland specified by the thirteenth article of the Treaty of Utrecht, the
' French (unless in case of accidents) cannot land on the coasts appertaining to
' the English in the Gulf of St. Lawrence, whether to dry their fish, or to
' spread their nets on the said coasts; but without these two exceptions the
' French shall be at liberty to fish, without molestation, in all parts of the said
' Gulf of St. Lawrence.

' With respect to the cession of the island of St. Pierre, the smallness of that
' island, and its situation near Plaisance, make the King of opinion that such a
' shelter will be illusory, and will rather serve to breed contests between the two
' nations, than to procure the accommodations for the fishery of the French sub-
' jects.

' The King had required the island of Cape Breton, or the island of St.
' John; his Majesty had even restrained himself to the little island of Conceau,
' and now makes the same proposition to his Britannic Majesty; or if the King of
' England, for reasons unknown to France, cannot agree to the cession of the
' isle of Conceau, it is proposed to add to the cession of St. Pierre, the islands of
' *Maquelon* or *Michelon*, two islands, of which one, which is St. Pierre, is but
' three leagues wide, and Michelon but two. However inconsiderable these two
' settlements may be, which do not properly make one, the King will accept of
' them, and will even oblige himself, 1. That neither in one or the other island,
' or in that of Conceau, if England cedes the latter, there shall be any military
' establishment; France will only maintain a guard of fifty men to enforce the
' police, which it will be necessary to maintain in those islands.

2. ' As far as possible, considering the weak guard of the police, the King
' will prevent all foreign vessels, even English, from landing at those Islands.

3. ' France does not pretend to fish and dry their fish on the Coast of New-
' foundland, but in pursuance of the stipulation of the 13th Article of the
' Treaty of Utrecht, provided it be understood that the French may fish and
' dry their fish on the Coasts of St. Pierre and Michelon.

4. ' Lastly, the King allows, that an English Commissary shall be resident in
' the said Island, to be witness to the punctuality with which the stipulated con-
' dition of the Treaty shall be observed.

' The partition of the four neutral Islands must be specified between the two
' Courts in the Preliminaries; France accepts the partition of those Islands pro-
' posed by England, provided that St. Lucia be declared to make part of the
' partition to be regulated in favour of France.

VI.

' The King, without entering into any discussion of the 6th Article, agrees
' to this Article as well as to the 7th.

H   VIII.

VIII.

' The King, with regard to the 8th Article, refers to the 7th Article of his *Ul-*
' *timatum.* It is not in his Majesty's power to evacuate countries, which apper-
' tain to his Ally the Empress Queen.

IX.

' The ninth Article of the Answer of England requires some explanation, for
' it is worded in such a manner as not to convey any precise meaning; it sup-
' poses respective Engagements on the part of the King towards the Empress,
' and on the part of England towards the King of Prussia, to which the two
' Courts are strangers. France does not suppose that the King of England can
' hinder the Allies of his Crown, such as the Sovereigns of Hanover, Cassel,
' and Brunswick, from joining their forces with those of the King of Prussia;
' but without entering into a needless discussion, the King is resolved, for the
' sake of peace, to make the most important sacrifices, and at the same time un-
' alterably determined, to grant nothing in the future Treaty of Peace, which
' may be contrary to the stipulations he has entered into with his Allies. It is
' with their consent, and with mutual concert, that the King proposes to Eng-
' land, in relation to the war in Westphalia, the 10th Article of the Memorial
' of his Majesty's propositions, and the 7th and 13th Articles of the French
' *Ultimatum.* The King abides by these Articles in answer to the 8th and 9th
' Articles of the Answer of England; not refusing, nevertheless, to treat of
' any fresh propositions which England may make on these heads, which shall
' be communicated to his Majesties Allies, and to which his Majesty will listen,
' with the consent of the Empress, if they are not contrary to his Majesty's
' engagements with that Princess.

X.

' France is of opinion that her proposition in relation to the Captures in which
' the King's subjects are interested, are so just, that she abides by them, and re-
' fers to the 12th Article of his Propositions on that head.

XI.

' The King, after signing of the Treaty, even of the Preliminaries, will give
' a Declaration under his hand, to the King of England, by which his Majesty
' will declare that his intention never was to bring the Towns of Ostend and
' Nieuport under his dominion.

XII.

' Provided that the terms of the Cessation of Hostilities may not be prejudi-
' cial to either Crown, France will agree to them.

XIII.

' France adopts the Negotiation between the India Companies of the two
Nations, on condition that the Negotiation shall be concluded at the same time
with

' with that between the two Crowns, and to that effect, each company shall
' enter upon their Negotiation without delay, and shall name Commissaries for
' that purpose.'

XIV.

' This Article will meet with no difficulty.
' The Court of England will do justice to the considerable Accommodations
' which the Court of France has testified in this Memorial, towards a reconci-
' liation between the two Crowns.

It may he collected from this Memorial that the first Article of the English
Answer was granted in the full extent which the Court of London required ;
France only desired eighteen months, instead of a year, for the emigration.

By granting the first part of the second Article, which cedes the whole cur-
rent of the Ohio to England, France proposed in regard to the second point
of that Article, to agree upon the nations which should be reputed neutral
between Canada, Carolina, and Louisiana : This proposition was the more reasonable, because that by agreeing on this division of the possession of the two
nations, an equitable system was adopted, discussions about the limits were pre-
vented for the future, and France did not incur the risk of losing the colony of
Louisiana, whenever it pleased the Court of London to invade it.

England, in her answer, persisted in requiring France to name the possessions
which the king desired to have on the coast of Africa. The third Article satisfied that demand.

The King, in the fourth Article, agreed to the Demolition of Dunkirk, as far as it
was possible ; for it will not be practicable, as after the peace of Utrecht, to erect
afresh a dam against the sea, which would inevitably carry it away presently. As
to what remained, it was offered to demolish every thing at Dunkirk which
had the appearance of a military port. Every one must be sensible how morti-
fying such a demolition must have been to France.

They agreed that the liberty of fishing in the Gulf of St. Laurence, and upon
the banks and coasts of Newfoundland, should be the compensation for the Demolition of Dunkirk. They accepted the cession of the Isle of St. Pierre, on
Conditions more than burthensome : the union of Michelon to St. Pierre was of
the least consequence, and the D. de Choiseul even assured Mr. Stanley that such
a cession would not be insisted on.

It is true the King rejected the inspection of the English Admiral, and that his
Majesty was resolved rather to refuse the Possession of St. Pierre, than to agree
to such an inspection, which was useless for the maintaining the stipulations of
the Treaty, and injurious to the dignity of the French nation, as that condition
seemed to be proposed only with a view to manifest, on the part of England, an
ill-timed superiority.

The other Articles of the French Memorial explain of themselves, with sufficient precision, the sincere and pacific intentions of his Majesty.

The eighth and ninth Articles of the Answer of England, could not be agreed
to in the form they stood ; they required at least, especially the last, some explanation : For how could the King cause Germany to be evacuated by his

forces,

forces, and at the same time fulfil his engagement with the powers of the Empire his Allies? There was a manifest contradiction in this proposition. One might suppose that England intended, by the ninth Article, that France, after having evacuated Westphalia, should be at liberty to dispatch forces into Bohemia or Saxony to the aid of the Empress Queen. But not to mention that such a march would have been as difficult as destructive to the King's army, is it probable that his Majesty, however closely he may be connected with that Princess, should abandon his possessions in Germany, conquered from his real Enemies, to march his armies at a distance from his frontiers, without any communication, send his troops to the aid of this Ally, and make war upon the King of Prussia, who is not his direct enemy!

Such nevertheless was the proposition of England. The King, in his Memorial, repeated what he had said before, that the two Crowns should equally remain at peace in Germany, as in the other parts of the world, or that England should propose some plain and honourable method to conciliate his Majesty's good faith towards his Allies, with his Majesty's desire of contributing no farther to the war in Germany.

M. de Bussy remitted the Memorial of the 9th of September to Mr. Pitt, on the 13th of the same month, and without having received any answer to that Memorial on the part of the British Court, Mr. Stanley wrote to the D. de Choiseul the following Letter, and received the Answer underneath on the same day.

No. XXX.

Mr. Stanley's Letter to the Duke de Choiseul, of the 20th September, 1761.

SIR,

'I Have the honour to inform your Excellency, pursuant to the orders I received yesterday from my Court, that as the Court of France has not agreed to accept the Propositions contained in the last Answer from the British Court, the King my Master has ordered me to request a passport of you, to return to England; my Court expects also, that M. Bussy will, on his part, receive the same orders.

' As the state of war has no influence over the personal sentiments of the King of England, with regard to their Most Christian Majesties, he is persuaded that they will take part in the event of his marriage, and I have letters in my hands by which he communicates that happy event to their Majesties. I have the honour to send your Excellency the copies, and I take the liberty, Sir, to consult your better intelligence, to inform myself of the most suitable manner of remitting these Letters, in pursuance of my Credentials, and according to the established custom of your Court.

' I have the honour to be, &c.
' Signed Stanley.

No. XXXI.

No. XXXI.

The Duke de Choiseul's Answer to Mr. Stanley, the 20th September, 1761.

SIR,

' THE King has ordered me, Sir, to expedite the paſsports which are neceſ-
' ſary for your return to England : you will find them annexed. M. Buſſy
' had orders to demand an Eclairciſſment with reſpect to the laſt Anſwer from
' England, and to return to France if thoſe Eclairciſſements were not favourable.
' They have certainly been otherwiſe, ſince your Court has anticipated his re-
' turn by your recall. However it be, Sir, his Majeſty hopes that ſome more
' happy opportunity will produce more effectual inclinations to peace, and he
' has charged me to obſerve to you, that you may aſſure the King of England,
' that he will always find him diſpoſed to renew the Negotiation, and to conſent
' to equitable conditions, which may eſtabliſh a firm union between the two
' Crowns.
' The King moſt ſincerely takes part in the marriage of the King of Eng-
' land; if you will ſend me the Letters from his Britiſh Majeſty, I will remit
' them to their Majeſties.

' I have the honour to be, &c.
' Signed Le Duc de Choiſeul.'

At the ſame time M. de Buſſy underſtood at London, that a Courier had been
diſpatched to recal Mr. Stanley, he explained himſelf on that occaſion; and after the Britiſh Miniſtry had confirmed the fact, he deſired, agreeable to the
orders he had received, the neceſſary Paſsports to return to France.

Thus the Negotiation between the two Crowns has been broken off. They
who talk ſo readily, and upon all occaſions, that *We muſt make Peace*, do
not conſider, that however well diſpoſed a Sovereign may be for the re-eſtabliſhment of tranquillity, his deſire cannot be effectual, but when it is equally
ſincere on the part of the other Belligerant Powers; and it will be admitted, on
reading this Memorial, that the King has omitted nothing to come to an Accommodation; no one can ſay, that his Majeſty's Allies have occaſioned the
rupture of the Negotiation. It has been proved, that the war which the King
maintains in Weſtphalia, is a war purely Engliſh, that it brings no advantage
either to the Empreſſes, or to Sweden, or to Saxony; beſides, the Propoſition
made by France, not to afford any ſuccours, either direct or indirect, to her
Allies in Germany, evidently demonſtrates that the war in Weſtphalia neither
has been, or could be, an impediment to the Peace.

England and ſome other courts would pretend that the engagements of the
King with his Catholic Majeſty, and the propoſition made by France to conciliate the differences of Spain with England at the ſame time with thoſe which were
the principal object of the Negotiation, had ſo diſguſted the court of London,
that for that reaſon only ſhe refuſed the terms for the concluſion of peace. It
is true, as has been ſhewn already, that the Britiſh Miniſter haughtily rejected

2

the

the expedient which his Majesty's prudent precaution induced him to suggest to England, with a view to conclude a firm peace, and to entirely obviate all obstacles which might oppose the continuance of that tranquillity which his Majesty laboured to re-establish; it is true likewise, that since the first Memorial of France, there was no farther notice of the differences of Spain in the proposition made by the Court of Versailles to that of London: his Catholic Majesty has even declared to the King, that if the objects which concerned the Spanish Monarchy should embarrass the negotiation and retard the peace, he agreed that those points should be no farther negotiated on the part of his Majesty. In fact, to repeat it once more, since the first Memorial of France, there has been no more mention of Spain. It cannot be imagined therefore, that the interests of his Majesty's Allies have proved an obstacle to the pacification. It remains therefore to examine whether the Negotiation has been broken off with respect to the articles which are the subjects of the particular discussion between the two Crowns.

It is necessary to recollect here, agreeable to the representation in the opening of the Memorial, what were the possessions acquired since the commencement of the war between the two Crowns, to the time when the Negotiation was entered upon, on the basis of the *Uti possidetis*.

England had conquered from France in North America, Canada, and the isles Royal and St. John, situate in the Gulf of St. Laurence: in South America, the isles of Guadaloupe and Marigalante: in Africa, Senegal, and the island of Goree: in Asia, Pondicherry and the French settlements on the coast of Coromandel.

In Europe, the island of Belle-isle, attacked since the opening of the Negotiation, and subsequent to the epochs of *statu quo*, proposed by the Court of France.

The *Uti possidetis* of France comprized in Asia, the English settlements on the coast of Sumatra, and other advantages on the side of the Mogul, of which they had yet received but imperfect accounts. In Europe, the island of Minorca, the Landgraviate of Hesse, the country of Hanau, and the town of Gottingen in the Electorate of Hanover. Lastly, France had re-established, or could have availed herself of the liberty which the infraction of the Treaty of Utrecht gave her, to re-establish the port of Dunkirk.

The King offered to guaranty Canada to the English in the utmost extent which the Court of London required.

His Majesty proposed that the right of fishing and of drying their fish on the Coast and on the Banks of Newfoundland should be confirmed to France, and on that condition she consented to the Demolition of Dunkirk.

The King proposed to restore the island of Minorca to England, for the cession of Guadaloupe and Marigalante.

His Majesty agreed to evacuate Hesse, the County of Hanau, and Gottingen, provided that one of the two Settlements she had lost in Africa were restored to her.

The Indian companies of the two nations were to treat concerning their particular pacification, agreeable to their reciprocal interests.

If

If the reduction of Belle-Isle should be acknowledged a legal conquest, though undertaken after the proposition of *Uti possidetis*, France agreed that the possession of that important island should remain to England.

Who can pretend to say, after the foregoing representation, that France has not scrupulously pursued, in all her propositions, the principle of her Memorial of the 26th of March! Can any one, at the same time, deny that the compensations offered by the King, were not as advantageous for England as she could desire?

Therefore it evidently follows, that the Allies of France in Germany could have been no obstacle to the peace, since they take no part in the war which is carried on in Westphalia, nor are assisted by the King's forces in the war maintained in Saxony, Silesia, and Pomerania. Moreover, it was proposed to England, on the part of France, that the two Courts should absolutely withdraw themselves from the war.

It is equally demonstrable, that Spain cannot be alledged to have been an impediment to the pacification, as the King did not renew the Proposition he made to unite the accommodation of the differences of that Crown with the Treaty under Negotiation between the Courts of Versailles and London, and his Catholic Majesty approved of their silence in this behalf.

It is certain, that the conditions and compensations offered by France, for the conclusion of a separate Peace with England, are all for the advantage of the latter Power; that the Court of London, had she been inclined to Peace, could not make claims beyond her Conquests; and that the Court plainly and clearly gave up every thing which was not compensated by some restitution on her part.

This detail necessarily leads to the question, which the whole universe, that suffers by the miseries of war, must necessarily make: What then has been the motive of the rupture of such an important Negotiation? That motive has no other principle than the positive aversion of the Court of London to Peace: it has proved impossible to infuse a conciliating spirit into a Court resolved to perpetuate the War, and less influenced by the real interests of the kingdom and the destruction of the human species, than inflated with the success she has had, and greedy of those advantages she has farther in view.

It is with regret that the King finds himself obliged to continue an opposition by force to the progress of the ambitious designs of his enemies, and under an impossibility of procuring his people that repose which his Majesty wished, for their welfare. The King trusts, that Providence will disappoint those vast projects, which England scarce endeavours to disguise, and which threaten the security of every Potentate. His Majesty, invariable in his pacific dispositions, will be always ready to concur in every expedient which may be judged proper to re-establish the public tranquillity, and will make no difficulty of sacrificing, even his own interests, to the glory and consolation of restoring Peace to his kingdom and to Europe.

By Order of the King,

Signed LE DUC DE CHOISEUL

C O N-

CONTENTS.